S0-BFI-749

The Right To Be Informed

Censorship in the United States

GERALD S. SNYDER

photographs

Julian Messner
New York

Published by Julian Messner,
a Division of Simon & Schuster, Inc.,
A Gulf+Western Company,
1 West 39th Street, New York, N.Y. 10018.
All rights reserved.

Copyright © 1976 by Gerald S. Snyder

Library of Congress Cataloging in Publication Data

Snyder, Gerald S
   The right to be informed.

   Bibliography: p. 187
   Includes index.
   1. Censorship—United States. I. Title.
Z658.U5S59   098'.12'0973   76-16191
ISBN 0-671-32809-3 lib. bdg.

Printed in the United States of America

THE RIGHT TO BE INFORMED
Censorship in the United States

As American society has changed and become more complex, and values and attitudes toward sex, women, religion, minority groups, schools, and government institutions have undergone radical revision, visual and written expressions once looked upon as vulgar are now commonplace. As a result of this new "freedom," book protests and burnings are flaring up; stricter controls on pornographic bookstores and theaters are being demanded; and school discussions of controversial subjects are being criticized.

This book looks into every area of censorship: books under attack, censoring violence on television, movies and pornography, censorship and the press, students' rights, censorship and the facts of life, and government as censor. Numerous examples and illustrations emphasize the sensitive, highly charged atmosphere surrounding the censorship question. Incredible stories of book burnings and school closings are compelling evidence of the strong emotional response censorship provokes. A clear-cut, thorough discussion of what obscenity is and how the courts have come to define it forms the basic foundation for this well-rounded calm presentation.

The Right to be Informed reveals that censorship is not an abstract thing, but rather is a powerful force to be reckoned with, by each and every one of us.

OFFICIALLY WITHDRAWN-SALE COPY

BOOKS BY GERALD S. SNYDER

THE RIGHT TO BE INFORMED
Censorship in the United States

THE RIGHT TO BE LET ALONE
Privacy in the United States

In Memory of My Mother

ACKNOWLEDGMENTS

For permission to excerpt and reprint copyrighted material, and to quote individuals, the author and publisher are grateful to the following:

Action for Children's Television
The American Scholar
Art Buchwald
Christianity and Crisis
  for excerpt from an article by Arthur J. Moore, August 18, 1975.
Columbia Broadcasting System, Inc.
Columbia Journalism Review
Da Capo Press
  for excerpt from *The Face on the Cutting Room Floor* by Murray Schumach. Copyright © 1964 by Murray Schumach.
Harper and Row, Publishers, Inc.
  for excerpt from *Books and the Teen-age Reader* by G. Robert Carlsen. Copyright © 1967 by G. Robert Carlsen.
Herb Jacobs, president, TelCom Associates, Inc.
Alfred A. Knopf, Inc.
  for excerpts and photograph from *The CIA and the Cult of Intelligence* by Victor Marchetti and John D. Marks. Copyright © 1974 by Victor L. Marchetti and John D. Marks.

St. Martin's Press, Inc.

for excerpt from *Lobbying for Freedom: A Citizen's Guide to Fighting Censorship at the State Level* by Kenneth P. Norwick.

Harold Matson Company, Inc.

for reproduction of a page from *I Saw The Fall of the Philippines* by Carlos P. Romulo. Copyright © 1943 by Carlos P. Romulo.

McGraw-Hill Book Company

for excerpt from *Soul on Ice* by Eldridge Cleaver. Copyright © 1968 by Eldridge Cleaver.

National Council of Teachers of English

The New York Times

for excerpt from an article by John B. Oakes. Copyright © 1975 by The New York Times Company. Reprinted by permission.

Newsweek

for excerpts from "Those (Bleep) TV Censors," September 9, 1974. Copyright © 1974 by Newsweek, Inc. All rights reserved. Reprinted by permission.

The Progressive

for excerpt from an article by Reo M. Christenson. Copyright © 1970, the Progressive, Inc.

The Sacramento Bee

Simon and Schuster, Inc.

for excerpt from *Fahrenheit 451* by Ray Bradbury.

The Washington Star

A Word from the Author

To enter into a discussion of the sensitive and complex issue of censorship is like stepping into an emotional minefield: one false step, one wrong or controversial statement made, and intense personal feelings are aroused; almost everyone seems to have an opinion on censorship. In this book I have tried to avoid a partisan viewpoint, aiming neither to condemn nor to glorify particular points of view, but, instead, to contribute simply to an *understanding* of censorship.

If I have taken any wrong turns, the responsibility is mine. For helping me to avoid most of the hazards, I especially would like to thank: Association for Supervision and Curriculum Development; Office for Intellectual Freedom of the American Library Association (ALA); Sex Information and Education Council of the United States (SIECUS); National Council of Teachers of English (NCTE); National Education Association (NEA); American Civil Liberties Union (ACLU); Action for Children's Television (ACT); American As-

sociation of State Colleges and Universities; Encyclopaedia Britannica Educational Corporation; Association
of American Publishers (AAP); National Council for
the Social Studies; Motion Picture Association of America (MPAA); Citizens United for Responsible Education
(CURE); and Parents Who Care.

GERALD S. SNYDER

CONTENTS

"Congress shall make no law respecting an establishment of religion, or prohibiting the free exercise thereof; or abridging the freedom of speech, or of the press; or the right of the people peaceably to assemble, and to petition the Government for a redress of grievances."

—First Amendment to the Constitution

1

Books Under Attack

Onward they marched, on to the state capitol, proudly, angrily, their signs held high: "DOWN WITH TEXTBOOKS—UP WITH GOD!" "RECYCLE THE BOOKS AND THE BOARD OF EDUCATION!" "EVEN HILLBILLIES HAVE CONSTITUTIONAL RIGHTS!" "WHEN THE BOOKS GO OUT, THE KIDS COME BACK!" "I HAVE A BIBLE—I DON'T NEED THOSE DIRTY BOOKS!"

They were parents, the mothers and fathers of students in Upper Kanawha Valley, West Virginia, and they were marching in Charleston, adding their protests to support the 3,500 coal miners who had walked off their jobs on a wildcat strike; the pickets walking around businesses, industrial plants, and schools; the people who had refused to work on construction projects, in factories, and in chemical complexes; and the drivers and conductors who had brought buses and trains to a halt.

Incredibly, it wasn't a labor issue that had anything

15

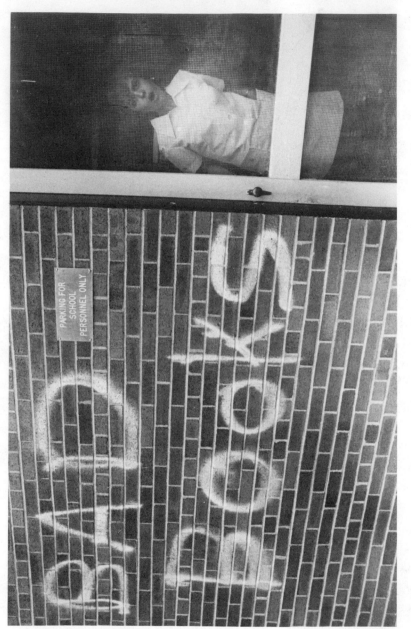

Book protesters' vandalism marks a Charleston, West Virginia, public grade school. (*William Tiernan*)

to do with all this. There was nothing about wages, or hours, or any of the other controversies that usually set off civil strife. The issue was *books,* mainly textbooks, that a wide segment of the people of Kanawha County felt were anti-Christian and anti-American, and not fit to be read. Before the protest was over, there were shootings and beatings, neighbor fighting neighbor, football games cancelled, schools bombed, dynamited, or vandalized.

As time would tell, this school-censorship "war" proved to be no irrational, isolated series of incidents, but the beginning of a movement, a farflung, coordinated protest by would-be censors and censorious groups. For in virtually all kinds of communities, large, small, rural, urban, sophisticated, affluent, and poor, there were cases of book bannings—in some places, book *burnings.*

Before peace finally settled over the narrow valleys and hillsides of Kanawha County, the National Knights of the Ku Klux Klan had joined in the fray, and the ultrarightist John Birch Society and other sophisticated, well-organized, right-wing extremists had taken up the issue. Repercussions from the 1974 "Battle of the Books," as the conflict was labeled, spread from school board to school board, state to state.

A Midwestern superintendent of public schools put it this way: "They may not use dynamite as they have in West Virginia, but there will be harassing phone calls in the middle of the night and obscene letters sent to your family, which are very upsetting."

While the controversy raged in Kanawha County, the

questionable books—some $500,000 worth—were removed from the shelves of the county's 121-school system, a review committee was appointed to decide which books should be returned, and another dissident group formed a separate splinter group when it found that it could not persuade the review committee to come out against the texts and other books it disliked. In a 500-page report, this second group released the names of scores of works it deemed objectionable, including Plato's *Republic*, Milton's *Paradise Lost* and *Paradise Regained*, Ernest Hemingway's *The Old Man and the Sea*, and Pearl Buck's *The Good Earth*.

In some communities across the country, teachers complained of being afraid to recommend books they felt necessary to their courses. School boards were intimidated. Librarians began to screen out controversial books more carefully, and some principals resigned out of a feeling of helplessness generated by the controversies. The resignation statement of the President of the Board of Education in Kanawha County included the following comments:

. . . We were faced with a situation verging on anarchy. The complete removal from the classroom of what I believed to be good books was more than I could accept. I further believed that to capitulate to mob rule would only encourage such action in the future. I still believe that these are good textbooks. They are not anti-Christian and anti-American as many people would have you believe.

In fact, our children have learned more about un-American and un-Christian behavior in the past few weeks from some of the adult population than the schools could teach in 12 years. I personally believe that the books which were adopted should be restored to the classrooms. . . .

Eventually, they were restored (to library shelves, for the most part, and not to the classrooms), but the controversy continued unabated—and coincided with new demands across the country for tougher anti-obscenity laws, and, as one observer put it, a "nationwide spasm of book-banning." Said one educator, her books under attack: "A teacher came to me the other day and asked 'What do you think? Can we defend teaching *this* in class?' She was talking about a unit in biology on the asexual reproduction of mollusks. It's really gotten that bad."

It's gotten so bad, says Judith F. Krug, director of the Office for Intellectual Freedom of the American Library Association (ALA) that "it's spreading across the country—I can only equate it with the McCarthy era." The recent controversies, she says, "are a manifestation of much more serious problems pervading the country—an anti-intellectualism brought on by a society so complex no one can hope to control it, let alone understand it." People feel helpless, she said, "and they find it's easier to censor school material than it is to express what's really bothering them. They say, 'If my kid didn't read *Go Ask Alice*, then the drug problem would go away.'" But the drug problem won't go away, she said, adding that the real danger is that the fears and frustrations of people are ripe for the manipulations of extremist groups out to take advantage of people and use them for political ends.

As an example of how extremist propaganda played on the controversy—to enflame passions and exploit fears—consider the following objections voiced by censorious groups in West Virginia.

- *The Supreme Court took prayer out of the public schools, but the books contain prayers and stories about religions; thus, they are violating the Supreme Court decision.*
- *The publication of the books and their introduction into the schools are part of a communist plot to undermine the morals of the nation's youth— the first step in the communist conspiracy to take over the nation itself.*

To the first charge, educators answered that there is a great deal of difference between teaching religion in the schools and teaching *about* religion. As U.S. Supreme Court Justice William Brennan has said: "The holding of the Court today plainly does not foreclose teaching about the Holy Scriptures or about the differences between religious sects in classes in literature or history. Indeed, whether or not the Bible is involved, it would be impossible to teach meaningfully many subjects in the social sciences or the humanities without some mention of religion."

As for the "communist plot" theory, the National Education Association (NEA) replied: "To accuse American textbook publishers—one of the most highly competitive participants in the American system of free enterprise—of taking part in a communist plot to overthrow this very system is such a self-contradictory allegation that it defies rational response."

Violence. Crime. A breakdown of morals. All of these may be found in the United States. But, complain the defenders of the controversial textbooks, the texts are blamed for these conditions, as though they are the *cause* of them, when in fact they merely are *reflectors* of them. The question is: Is it the books themselves that corrupt or do the books merely mirror a society that in some way is "corrupting?" A defender of the textbooks used in West Virginia observed: "They help prepare kids to take on life as it is, which isn't exactly like we want it to be."

Dr. Helen D. Wise, former president of the National Education Association, spoke out in stronger terms: "How can we teach our children about democracy and free speech when we burn the books we do not like and have teachers arrested for assigning unpopular material?"

The Authors League of America, echoing this feeling, asserted that students do not need to be protected from the language in books, but from "these hysterical, childish assaults by 'adults' on the fundamental freedoms guaranteed by the First Amendment, the freedom to read and freedom to teach." "What are parents afraid of?" demanded one author. "Children can go into any paperback book shack, any corner drugstore, and pick up cheap, poorly written $1.25 novels that are sprinkled with 'dirty' words that would make a Marine or truck-driver blush."

In what may be termed a summing up of the anti-censorship viewpoint, a Baptist minister, the Rev. Thomas A. Conley, told a Maryland school board that had attempted to set up a board of censors to review classroom materials: "To eliminate ideas and ideologies with which we don't agree is arbitrary and undermines the heart of a democracy in which personal and indi-vidual choice must decide what is right and proper for

Charleston High School students demonstrate in support of controversial textbooks. (William Tiernan)

its perusal and use as well as for the use of that individual's children."

So goes the furor set off by the new wave of book bannings. But even if the controversy dies down, it will not die out, for the issue raises this basic question: What is the purpose of the American educational system?

"To provide the Three Rs," is the obvious answer. But, most educators would agree, it is also to give young people the skills needed to function in a highly complex society, and to broaden intellectual tools needed to cope with the problems of today.

"Maybe," answer the textbook critics, "but *these* books, they dwell on the morbid. They have too much about prostitution, too much about dope addiction, too much about racism, too much about death, too much emphasis on four-letter gutter words." These books, they say, "take God's name in vain."

At the same time, it must be noted that not all of the groups that take this position are ban-the-books groups, but groups that earnestly feel that books must be screened for "objectionable" material, notably explicit sexual passages and racial references.

The West Virginia protesters were sincere in their beliefs. They did not look upon themselves as censors. They saw these books as somehow sacrilegious or in some way against God.

According to many press accounts, they are poor, downtrodden hillbillies, living in narrow hillsides, coves, valleys, and coal camps. It is much closer to the truth, however, that they are a people with a distinctive cultural tradition—a "hill culture"—with a heritage that goes back to the English frontier in Ireland and the lowland Scots, who, in America's immigrant days, came to the valleys and hills of Appalachia. There they cleared the fields, developed their own schools, churches, and stores, and generally lived a life independent of large towns or cities. Living with the principle that "blood is thicker than water," they remained aloof in their attitudes and beliefs, always refusing to compromise, distrusting strangers, preferring face-to-face interaction with those who were known to them.

It is no wonder then that a people with this background would find themselves alienated from a sudden new flow of multicultural and multi-ethnic ideas such as were found in the controversial textbooks. To the people of Appalachia, the new ideas attacked their own traditional, long-standing values, and therefore were "blasphemous," "obscene," and "unpatriotic."

These people were not all "hillbillies," or uneducated people—many were very educated—but they could not understand why the public schools would not echo *their* beliefs, why *their* values were constantly being scorned. They were caught up in the changes being made in society. As one observer explained: "They see their children watching things on TV that are very different from the way they believe and they see their children reflecting some of the things which they hear in popular music. They feel that those areas are far out of their control, but that the taxes they pay for the schools are close at hand and they are going to get those textbooks out of the classroom."

Other individuals offer other reasons for defending censorship. For example, one well-known professor spoke for many individuals when he said that freedom from censorship has gotten out of hand, producing: "a world in which homosexual rape is simulated on the stage, in which the public flocks to witness professional fornication, in which New York's Times Square has become a hideous marketplace for printed filth."

The professor asserted:

> . . . It seems to me that the cultural market in the United States today is awash in dirty books, dirty movies, dirty theater. Our cultural condition has not improved as a result of the new freedom. I'll put it bluntly: if you care for the quality of life in our American democracy, then you have to be for censorship.

In the simplest definition, to censor means "to suppress," and for some typical cases generated by different forms of suppression, consider the following:

- In Drake, North Dakota, the school board ordered the school janitor to burn Kurt Vonnegut's anti-war novel *Slaughterhouse-Five*, along with James Dickey's *Deliverance*, and copies of *Short Story Masterpieces*—all because of the "language" in them.

- For the same reason, parents tried (unsuccessfully) to remove *Ms.* magazine from a library in Bennington, Vermont.
- In Junction City, Kansas, members of a church burned copies of *Playboy* magazine and the book *The Exorcist*.
- In South Carolina, a high school teacher was arrested and charged with the distribution of obscene material to minors—for recommending *Slaughterhouse-Five*.
- In Prince William County, Virginia, some 500 people crowded a Manassas high school auditorium to hear 15 speakers condemn a controversial textbook series as "degrading religion," containing "gutter language," and "dwelling on morbid aspects of death." The one speaker who spoke out in defense of the books was continually interrupted by catcalls from the audience.
- In Hillsborough, New Hampshire, a group of aroused parents started a campaign against obscenity after a student brought home from a library a copy of David Dalton's *Janis*, a biography of the late rock singer Janis Joplin. Proclaimed the parents: "Why should taxpayers money be used to buy obscene books and books with obscene language in them?"
- *Invisible Man,* Ralph Ellison's 1952 National Book Award winner, was banned by the school board in St. Francis, Wisconsin, after a number of par-

ents complained that it contained "objectionable material."

- In Syracuse, Indiana, a small group of parents, complaining that John Steinbeck's classic *Of Mice and Men* contained "cuss words," forced the local high school to ban the book.
- At the prestigious Smithsonian Institution in Washington, D.C., Secretary S. Dillon Ripley directed the cancellation of a lecture by poet and novelist Erica Jong, author of the sexually explicit novel *Fear of Flying*. Jong withdrew from the lecture before it could be cancelled, charging the Smithsonian with trying to censor her lecture in advance.

As dramatic as these examples are, they are being called by certain educators and libertarians exercises in futility, battles by censorious groups or individuals against inevitability—acts, as one observer put it, that are "reminiscent of the French peasants of the early 19th Century who resisted textile machinery by throwing their wooden shoes into the gears of mechanical looms, or of the Luddites of England who saw sabotage as the only answer to the spinning jenny."

They are examples, in other words, of demonstrations against change, efforts to hold back modernity, to defy, for instance, the intense lifestyles of the popular music world, in which almost every subject is sung about —topics ranging over a whole world of startling new attitudes toward women, minority groups, religion, government institutions, and numerous other elements of society. As the textbooks and other materials make clear, what once was regarded as vulgar is not necessarily so regarded today. In fact, the "vulgar" may be quite acceptable. People no longer are as shocked as they used to be about motherhood without marriage, for example, and homosexuals, among others, now publicly proclaim the right to be what they want.

The current controversies are legal. They are philosophical. They are sociological. And, it seems, they are never-ending.

Remove the offending books? Mollify the censors? In many instances, that has been the course taken. It is, however, a "most dangerous temptation," warns John Maxwell, Deputy Executive Secretary of the National Council of Teachers of English (NCTE). He asserts: "History is replete with examples to prove that such a strategy only whets the censors' appetites. Before they were done in Kanawha, the censors had proscribed, in addition to works by Poe, Thoreau, Hawthorne, and Eliot, such works as 'Pinocchio' and 'Three Billy Goats Gruff.' There is no end to what the censor can find objectionable. There is no work, no author, that will be safe from some censor, somewhere."

Some books have been condemned or banned for showing vivid scenes of Eskimos slaughtering caribou and cutting up fish, or depicting animals—such as wolves and foxes—appearing in human form. To some people,

"Good Lord" is viewed as a profanity, "What the heck!" as offensive slang.

It was the American newspaper columnist and critic Haywood Broun who said of censorship that just about everyone can be shown something that he or she thinks should be censored. (The extreme form of censorship, said the playwright George Bernard Shaw, is assassination.) But Stoddard King, a poet of the early twentieth century, probably expressed the anticensorship sentiment best when he wrote:

> *A writer owned an Asterisk,*
> *   And kept it in his den,*
> *Where he wrote tales (which had large*
> *   sales)*
> *   Of frail and erring men:*
> *And always, when he reached the point*
> *   Where carping censors lurk,*
> *He called upon the Asterisk*
> *   To do his dirty work.*

One example of censorship reasoning is shown by the objections to *The Dynamics of Language* textbook, and a statement in the book to the effect that "All first efforts are improved by revision." "Would this include the Ten Commandments?" some of the protesters in West Virginia asked. As another illustration, a story about David Glasgow Farragut (who said "Damn the torpedoes!" at Mobile Bay in 1864) was condemned for its "profanity."

One book for junior and senior high school students was accused of teaching disrespect for law and order by the presentation of a poem with these lines:

He took me around the corner
and he rang a little bell.
Along came a police car
and he took me to my cell.

It was clear that in West Virginia the protest had strong overtones of racism. In the new books there were the works of such black writers as Dick Gregory, James Baldwin, Malcolm X, Eldridge Cleaver, and Langston Hughes, and other books about blacks. "Get the Nigger Books out!" became a racist cry during the controversy. "Would you want your daughter to marry a black man?" demanded one irate parent of a Kanawha minister.

The antitextbook protesters replied that the "racial hatred" was in the books, not in the protests. However, one member of the main textbook review committee commented: ". . . not only was the racial issue an issue in this, but . . . another culture, another way of life. Ghetto stories about any race of people, stories outside our particular realm of experience, or outside our children's realm of experience, I think, elicited a great deal of criticism. Things that were not always pretty, things that we probably would not expect our children ever to experience were objected to."

When an NEA panel, invited to conduct hearings on the West Virginia controversy, asked a black minister if the adopted books accurately portrayed blacks in America, he replied yes, and interestingly had this to say:

One of the expressions of racism, to me, is the sub-tlety of how other folks have a way of choosing who is acceptable to you . . . I have had people say to me, personally, "I know that you would not want to accept Eldridge Cleaver or Malcolm X in a book to be taught to your child." And I would ask, "How do you know that?" And they would say, "Because they do not represent your people in the best light." Now, two assumptions were made there. One is that I would reject Malcolm and Eldridge and Angela (Davis). The other is that the light in

At the Board of Education in Charleston, West Virginia. *(William Tiernan)*

which they see them is the best light and the writers do not emerge very handsomely, or very American, in that light. Therefore, I should reject them.

It comes on to the point of racist notions like that —saying that not only do we decide certain things about what you do and where you go, but we also take the prerogative of choosing your heroes. And since these particular heroes are not acceptable to us, they should not be acceptable to you . . . And I think that those kinds of statements and the unacceptability of certain kinds of writers are an expression of a subtle racism.

One other point that I find very interesting now is that some of my white ministerial colleagues accept Martin Luther King, Jr., as a patriot. When in his lifetime he took the position on the Vietnam War that he did, almost from every mountainside he was being declared unpatriotic.

About these undercurrents of racism, the Teachers Rights Division of the NEA responded:

The situation in Kanawha County presents an extreme, but microcosmic, picture of the cultural conflict that now, as in many troubled eras of the past, threatens to destroy the academic freedom of the classroom in communities across the nation. At this particular juncture in history, it poses another threat to rights that have been newly won: the right of racial and ethnic minority groups to be included in the textbooks, and the right of all students to learn that in the world and in this society, white is not always right; that white, middle-class values are not the only, nor even always the best, values; and that the history of the United States is not one long, unblemished record of Christian benevolence and virtue. Teaching and learning these truths are not acts of subversion or irreligion. But to ignore them is an act of blind patriotism and religious bigotry.

Throughout history, there has been controversy about public school textbooks. And the current controversy will continue. As long as the public shows concern about the results of schooling, as long as textbooks and other materials become involved with religion, morals, politics, and sex, and as long as teachers and other school professionals keep delving into controversial areas in the classroom, seeking to deepen or change the values and attitudes of their students, there will be controversy.

Throughout the country antitextbook hardliners will cry out for years to come that the "anti-Christian" and "filthy" textbooks must go, while others will plead with equal conviction: Shouldn't teachers have an absolute right to exercise their professional judgment about what they think are appropriate books and materials to use in the classroom? Why should a minority of parents have the right to impose their judgment on what is "fit read-

A textbook protester. (William Tiernan)

ing matter"? By what right should individual parents have the power to veto books, films, or other material used in the public schools?

The real tragedy of all the upheaval is not just that there are no "right" or "wrong" answers to these questions, which indeed there are none, but that the most serious victims of the protests are not those who raise the questions or attempt to answer them—parents, teachers, or school officials—but the students. As more and more material becomes "questionable," as more review committees are formed, and as more and more textbooks are taken out of the schools, there will be a disruption of curriculums and, for some students, a disruption of future educational plans.

Yet probably, it is not the disruptions themselves that are most important, but what they stand for.

A Kanawha County citizen summed it up: "It's a matter of principle—you've got to hold on to the principles that you believe in."

2

What Is Obscenity?
The Courts Can't Decide

"Fornication!" . . . "Masturbation!" . . . "Flagellation!"
. . . "Nipples!" It was a crowded session on censorship, during a convention of the National Association of
College Stores, and the bookstore managers expressed
surprise at the frank words uttered by the speaker. Yet
no one was shocked. No one labeled any of these words
"obscene" or offensive—words which in another day,
another age, before another audience, no one even would
have dared whisper.

But this was 1975, and the managers, all wary of the
pressures being put upon them by pressure groups not
to sell certain books, merely listened carefully as the
speaker warned them of censorship bills that threatened
to ban from bookstores and libraries such popular titles
as *Catch-22*, *The Catcher in the Rye*, *The Grapes of
Wrath*, *The Naked Ape*, and *Slaughterhouse-Five*. Of
one such bill, vetoed by the governor of Pennsylvania
at the very last moment, the speaker said: "Any private
citizen could have walked into a bookshop and decided

that it was selling an obscene book. All copies of the title could have been confiscated immediately and the store owner charged with a criminal act."

At the very heart of the current censorship controversy lies the question of what constitutes obscenity. For in all of the titles mentioned above, there are certain words, certain phrases, and descriptions of certain situations which their critics would unreservedly label "obscene" or "pornographic."

What *is* obscenity? What *is* pornography? Both are crimes in every state, yet the nation's courts have tied themselves into knots trying to define them, because, in truth, there is no single definition of either.

Then, too, perhaps even more important than the issue of defining obscenity or pornography is the question of where the First Amendment freedoms of expression end when it comes to obscene literature, motion pictures, plays, and other forms of expression. Are these freedoms absolute, or do they indeed have an ending? Granted that we can arrive at some agreement on what obscenity is, are all forms of obscenity to be tolerated?

We'll attempt some answers to these complex questions; but first, down to the business of definitions. The Supreme Court uses the terms "obscenity" and "pornography" synonymously, both referring to descriptions of sex-related subjects. But generally, "obscene" is the broader term, referring to anything that is indecent, disgusting, or grossly offensive. It has been defined from time to time, for example, as "anything that would corrupt the most corrupted individual of the community," or "anything that is lewd and revealing, exposing parts of the body," or "anything that is offensive to modesty or decency." In one of the most famous obscenity cases, the 1934 *United States v. One Book Entitled Ulysses* case, obscene was held to mean "tending to stir the sex impulse or to lead to sexually impure and lustful thoughts."

"Pornography," the companion term, the one most often linked to obscenity, deals strictly with materials pertaining to sex. In common usage, it means "a depiction (as in writing or painting) of licentiousness or lewdness: a portrayal of erotic behavior designed to cause sexual excitement."

The trouble, however, with trying to define obscenity

New York City's "Porno Strip"—42nd Street near Seventh Avenue—has been at the center of controversy between police and theater owners who charge censorship. *(Donal F. Holway)*

and pornography is that both terms are too general, too all-embracing, and too imprecise. Most important, however, both terms are *subjective*, meaning different things to different people. Who can define a "corrupted individual?" Who is to say what is or is not "lewd" or "revealing?" What one person or one group has the right to determine what is "offensive" to all people? The fact is that what may be lewd to one person may not be to another. What is offensive to one individual may be quite acceptable to another. And the problem is compounded by geography. For instance, the movie *Carnal Knowledge* may be considered obscene in a southern rural town. But in the center of the thriving borough of Manhattan in New York, or in Chicago or San Francisco, it may be viewed as quite acceptable and positively harmless.

A person could take a copy of the controversial *Fanny Hill* and, moving from county to county in a single state, would find it deemed a piece of obscenity in one county, a work of art in another.

As Frederick vanPelt Bryan, the U.S. District Court Judge who in 1959 made one of the most historic obscenity decisions in this country's history—ruling that the unexpurgated version of the novel *Lady Chatterley's Lover* by the British novelist D.H. Lawrence was not obscene and could not be banned from the U.S. mails—stated: "There have been enormous shifts in the standard of sexual mores. It has made it most difficult for the courts to deal with because we are dealing with what offends current standards. What may be offensive to residents of a small rural community would be not at all offensive to the more sophisticated residents of a larger city."

The courts, in short, have been attempting to define the indefinable. And the reason they go on trying is simply because so many censorship questions swirl around the charge, "It's obscene!" "It's pornographic!"

For years, the courts and the best legal minds, including those on the Supreme Court, have struggled, and failed, to define obscenity (or pornography) so that a definition can be used in cases of censorship. Much worse, as one observer noted, "They will continue to fail, for like beauty, obscenity is in the eye of the beholder." According to the late High Court Justice John Marshall Harlan, this "intractable problem" (of finding a definition) has "produced a variety of views among the members of the Supreme Court unmatched in any other course of constitutional adjudication." Added the late Justice Hugo L. Black: "No person, not even the most learned judge, much less a layman, is capable of knowing in advance" what the High Court will decide about obscenity. Furthermore, as the former Justice William O. Douglas—the Court's "Great Dissenter"—has said, in trying to define obscenity, "the nation is getting into a morass."

Obscenity, therefore, remains a very murky area of the law. Yet for all the difficulty presented by any attempt to construct an acceptable definition—"it is impossible to construct any meaningful and constitutional definition," as one lawyer bluntly stated—the courts feel compelled to go on trying. For as long as there are censorship cases, and questions arising from acts of censorship, there will be the need to understand more deeply the complex issue of obscenity.

The courts realize that rather than continue to search in vain for a simple definition, they are better off setting down certain tests and guidelines.

In 1957 the turning point came in *Roth v. United States*, the first case in the history of the Supreme Court to face up to the basic constitutionality of obscenity laws.

This landmark case, called simply "Roth" in legal parlance, arose when Samuel Roth, a publisher of books, photographs, and magazines was convicted in the lower courts of mailing obscene circulars and advertising matter and an obscene book. In upholding the decision, the Supreme Court ruled for the first time that obscenity is *not* protected by the First Amendment.

The First Amendment, the High Court declared, did not protect sexual materials which combined the elements of "prurience" and worthlessness. "Implicit in the history of the First Amendment," the Court said, "is the rejection of obscenity as utterly without redeeming social importance."

In other words, the Court was saying, what is obscene may be legally censored. So for the first time in the history of the United States the *worth* of material became a factor in determining the constitutional protection to be granted to a means of communication.

It is important to note that the Court took this step

while continuing to grant constitutional protection to ideas. "All ideas," as Justice William J. Brennan said in the majority decision, "having even the slightest redeeming social importance—unorthodox ideas, controversial ideas, even ideas hateful to the prevailing climate of opinion—have the full protection of the guarantees" of the First Amendment.

Sexual material was ruled no exception. The High Court upheld the constitutionality of anti-obscenity laws, but it did not bow down to those who would have *all* sexually-oriented material banned from the country. The Court declared:

> Sex and obscenity are not synonymous. Obscene material is material which deals with sex in a manner appealing to prurient interest. The portrayal of sex, e.g., in art, literature, and scientific works, is not itself sufficient reason to deny material the constitutional protection of freedom of speech and press. Sex, a great and mysterious force in human life, has indisputably been a subject of absorbing interest to mankind through the ages; it is one of the vital problems of human interest and public concern.

In *Roth*, the Supreme Court put forth its official test of obscenity: "Whether to the average person, applying contemporary community standards, the dominant theme of the material taken as a whole appeals to the prurient interest."

It was asserting, then, that material was obscene if it:

a) appealed to prurient interest.
b) was patently offensive under current community standards.
c) was utterly without any redeeming social value.

The guidelines were set. The trouble was, however, that no one, not even the courts that were to carry out the Supreme Court's ruling, could decide upon which kinds of sexually-oriented materials were really "obscene." After *Roth*, thousands of cases were decided across the country, but the years were marked by confusion: no one could agree on a single approach to obscenity, and writers and publishers and producers of plays never really knew what they could write or produce.

The courts and writers and others had the guidelines. But the meaning of the words in those guidelines was not clear. Did "prurient" mean merely shocking or, perhaps, did it mean "diseased?" Couldn't "patently offensive" in the view of one person be "patently inoffensive" to another person? Couldn't something that was "prurient" in the mind of one person be perfectly "healthy" in the mind of another? Clearly, the words were abstract, meaning different things to different people. In the minds of some people, the Vietnam War was "obscene."

Thus, even with *Roth*, the problem of understanding obscenity was nowhere near solved, not for other courts and not for the High Court itself. In one obscenity case (*Jacobellis v. Ohio*), the Court issued six separate opinions, with no more than two Justices in agreement. In another case, Justice Potter Stewart was moved almost in despair to remark of obscenity and demonstrate again the futility of trying to define it: "I know it when I see it."

Not until 1973 was an attempt made to clarify the confusing *Roth* guidelines. On June 21 of that year—in the most recent major decision on obscenity to date—the Supreme Court restricted the guidelines as the result of a case (*Miller v. California*) involving the conviction of one Marvin Miller for violating the obscenity law in California by distributing obscene material through the mails.

The High Court, by a 5-4 vote, rejected Miller's appeal and ruled that state obscenity laws do not automatically violate the First Amendment. The Court kept in effect the "appeal to prurient interest" and "patently offensive" tests formulated in the *Roth* case. But the Court said these tests must be applied with a view to *local* and not national community standards. Thus, it widened the latitude of states and municipalities to decide what is or is not obscene.

The new *Miller* guidelines, which to this day remain in effect, cite the following standards for determining obscenity:

a) Whether the average person applying contemporary community standards would find the work, taken as a whole, appeals to the prurient interest.

b) whether the work depicts or describes, in a patently offensive way, sexual conduct specifically defined by the applicable state law.
c) whether the work, taken as a whole, lacks serious literary, artistic, political, or scientific value.

What happened, in effect, was that the Supreme Court could not decide nationally what was obscene. So it told the communities to decide for themselves.

As it turned out, however, the communities experienced a hard time deciding, and the need to have to decide for themselves caused much divisiveness. Summing up the sense of frustration felt as a result of the Court's *Miller* ruling, Justice Douglas observed in a dissenting opinion: "Every author, every book-seller, every movie exhibitor and perhaps every librarian is now at the mercy of the local police force's conception of what appeals to 'prurient interest' or is 'patently offensive.'"

According to Justice Douglas: "The standards can vary from town to town and day to day in unpredictable fashion. How can an author or bookseller or librarian know whether the community deems his books acceptable until after the jury renders its verdict? If the magazines in question were truly 'patently offensive' to the local community, there would be no need to ban them through the exercise of police power; they would be banned by the marketplace which provided no buyers for them."

Because the important legal question concerning obscenity—what is the applicable "community" for determining community standards?—was not answered by the High Court in *Roth*, many lower courts have urged that a national community standard be devised.

The majority of Justices who made the 1973 ruling disagreed. In the words of Chief Justice Warren E. Burger:

> Under a national Constitution, fundamental First Amendment limitations on the powers of the States do not vary from community to community, but this does not mean that there are, or should or can be, fixed, uniform national standards of precisely what appeals to the prurient interest or is patently offensive. These are essentially questions of fact, and our nation is simply too big and too diverse for this Court to reasonably expect that such standards could be articulated for all 50 states in a single formulation, even assuming the prerequisite consensus exists . . . To require a state to structure obscenity proceedings around evidence of a national community standard would be an exercise in futility.

The point is, as Justice Burger went on to explain, that "it is neither realistic nor constitutionally sound to read the First Amendment as requiring that the people of Maine or Mississippi accept the public depiction of conduct found tolerable in Las Vegas or New York City."

Also, the critics claimed, it was all right to make immune from censorship works which had "serious literary, artistic, political, or scientific value," but why had the Court left unexplained any measure for defining this standard?

In many states, the difficulty of formulating a clear national standard has led police to form definitions of their own. In one city, for instance, the police chief warned merchants that they faced misdemeanor charges if they sold such magazines as *Playboy, Oui,* and *Penthouse.* "I am up here to uphold the standards of the community," he declared. "As their police chief, the people have entrusted me to decide what is obscene." Defining obscenity by asserting that "anything obscene humanly speaking is also obscene in a book," he explained that if it was illegal for a woman to appear in a state of undress, then any picture of a woman in such a state also is obscene.

Many judges, however, have refused to allow the 1973 High Court ruling to give police a completely free hand. In Hartford, Connecticut, for instance, Circuit Court Judge David J. Jacobs said it is not up to police to decide what is or is not obscene. Ruling in a case where a vendor's $3,000 stock of allegedly obscene magazines was seized by police, the judge decided in favor of the vendor and asserted that if police were to have their way, there would be "as many different standards of what constitutes obscenity as there are policemen."

Typical of the confusion in trying to figure out what is meant by "contemporary community standards" is what happened in Modesto, California, when the owner of an adult bookstore was charged with selling obscene material. The jury considering the case did consider the materials sold as obscene, but since between 50 and 150 persons a day went into the store, it ruled that the materials were not counter to "contemporary community standards." And the case was dismissed.

So pornography has continued to flourish. As a reporter for *The New York Times* summed it up: "What some legal experts thought would become a nationwide war on dirty books and movies as a result of the Court ruling has turned out to be a half-hearted skirmish. In most places residents appear to be apathetic. The police say they have more important crimes to fight. Many local prosecutors contend that they have neither the time nor the money to spend cracking down on smut dealers."

A Seattle police lieutenant complained: "The judges are talking out of both sides of their mouths at the same time. Who is the community the Supreme Court said has the power to decide what is pornography? If elected officials set up a censor board which says this is a dirty movie and illegal (he was talking about 'Deep Throat'), then the Supreme Court says, 'no, you can't do that.'"

Adding to the confusion, when the High Court ruled that state obscenity statutes must specifically define sexual conduct that cannot be shown "in a patently offensive way," many of the state statutes were challenged as unconstitutional because of their vagueness. Although Berger had suggested that "patently offensive" meant pictures or accounts of "ultimate sex acts, normal or perverted, actual or simulated" and "masturbation, excretory functions, and lewd exhibition of the genitals," the states were still in a quandary over what definition to accept. As a result, at least ten states declared their obscenity laws unconstitutional.

But sometimes the trouble was not that the statutes were too vague but that they were too explicit. The editor of a Winchester, Indiana, newspaper, for example, explained to the city councilmen that their new obscenity ordinance was so clearly formulated that he found it not fit to print. In Danvers, Massachusetts, an ordinance adopted by the selectmen was loaded with such comments as "sections *d* and *c* are unprintable," leaving one observer to comment: "It appears that scholars of jurisprudence may be called upon to solve a new problem: Can a law violate its own provisions."

The fact is, it appears, that obscenity may be whatever any court says it is. For the words used in the 1973 Supreme Court decision—"prurient," "patently offensive," "serious literary," "artistic," "average," and so forth—are themselves so vague as to be open to court interpretations. As one person has put it: "It is not possible to draw up a blacklist of words and situations as a sort of test to determine which books should come under censorship and which should not. The same words, the same situations that seem objectionable and extraneous in one book may be legitimate and valid in the next. We have not learned of any censorship group or agency able consistently to distinguish between the two."

Just take the word "average." This means, according to one dictionary, "typical, common, ordinary." But what do *those* words mean? When applied to a particular situation, the meaning of each one of those words may be open to interpretation. In his book *Lobbying For Freedom: A Citizen's Guide to Fighting Censorship at the State Level,* Kenneth P. Norwick comments on the reference to the mythical "average" person by stating: "As should be obvious, there really is no average when it comes to predicting the prurient appeal of any given book or film, and any requirement that the jury measure such appeal on such a person would clearly be an exercise in futility and/or sheer guesswork."

Furthermore, the communities have been caught up in debates over where, exactly, the line should be drawn. Lacking a clear definition of obscenity, some people believe that "hardcore" pornography is all right.

In a case decided by the Minnesota Supreme Court, upholding the conviction of a theater owner for showing the film *The Art of Marriage,* the jurists defined "hardcore" pornography as material "with no pretense of artistic value" and the "soft-cored" variety as being less offensive and protected by the Constitution as long as it is not sold to minors or shown to unwilling viewers.

The trouble with these definitions, however, is that even they are open to interpretation. When someone at a Freedom to Read Committee panel of the Association of American Publishers (AAP) offered as a definition of hardcore pornography, "the exploitation for profit of private pleasure," Kenneth McCormick of Doubleday, who was then the chairman of the committee, pointed out the inadequacy of the definition.

"I happen to enjoy chopping wood," he said. "That's one of my private pleasures."

Although few people can agree on where the difference between hard and softcore pornography lies, Jack Valenti, president of the Motion Picture Association of America (MPAA), has offered what may be the clearest definition: "Hardcore pornography means specific sexual acts performed on screen in full and vivid detail. Softcore means that the act of sexual intercourse remains unseen, while everything else is there. It's a fuzzy distinction but those in the trade know it."

On June 24, 1974, more Supreme Court decisions on obscenity were handed down; but they did nothing, or very little, to clear up the confusion over the issue. Using the *Miller* case as its guideline, the High Court ruled (in *Jenkins v. Georgia*) that "the film *Carnal Knowledge* is not obscene," and so overruled a 1972 conviction of a Georgia motion picture theater manager who had shown the film. Ruled Judge William Rehnquist: "It would be a serious misreading (of the *Miller* decision) to conclude that juries have unbridled discretion in determining what is 'patently offensive.'" The Court had seen the movie and declared:

While the subject matter of the picture is, in a broader sense, sex, and there are scenes in which sexual conduct including 'ultimate sexual acts' is to be understood to be taking place, the camera does not focus on the bodies of the actors at such times. There is no exhibition whatever of the actors' genitals, lewd or otherwise, during these scenes. There are occasional scenes of nudity, but nudity alone is not enough to make material legally obscene under the *Miller* standards.

Lack of a clear-cut definition for obscenity has not stopped prosecutors from pressing obscenity charges in the various states. Although many local statutes make no effort to define obscenity, the statutes are still taking effect. In 1974, for instance, the Arkansas Supreme Court upheld the conviction of a book seller for selling an alleged obscene book, observing that the Supreme Court has always held that the language of a statute is sufficient if it conveys a warning that can be understood. Justice Conley Byrd, however, who was one of the dissenting Arkansas judges, said the ruling in his state places every citizen at the mercy of loose interpretation. Any law enforcement official can now say what is or is not obscene, he said, and "that kind of vagueness should not exist in our criminal law enforcement."

Yet to some, the difficulty, or impossibility, of defining obscenity is a good thing. One well-known author in effect took this view when he said that "for the legislature or any county official to try and define obscenity is almost sure to encourage the vigilante morality and most assuredly to give publicity and notoriety to all sorts of cheap and boring books and movies which would otherwise go off to the anonymity they richly deserve."

What *is* obscenity?

Who really knows?

3

On Library Shelves:
The Right to Read

In Hillsville, Virginia, in 1975, the chairman of the Carroll County School Board showed up for a meeting one day carrying a brown paper bag containing copies of the *Encyclopedia of Witchcraft* and *Demonology and Their Craft*. He demanded to know: Who orders books for the library? Why should prayer be banned from public schools and "books like these" be permitted?

In city after city, library after library, similar questions are being posed today. "Would you want your daughter to read *God's Little Acre?*" "Are drugs, rape, abortion, homosexuality, suicide, unwed mothers, fit subjects for young adults to read about?" "Should teenagers be exposed to books with explicit sexual references?"

To these questions, more and more librarians, among others, are responding affirmatively, and, as a consequence, touching off arguments around the country. At no time in history have America's libraries been at the center of so much bitter controversy, as evidenced in

53

the following brief roundup of incidents that occurred in 1975 alone:

- *Brockton, Massachusetts.* J. D. Salinger's *The Catcher in the Rye* was voted removed from the city's junior high school library, but the book was retained in the high school library, along with *Catch-22, Manchild in the Promised Land,* and *Down These Mean Streets*—books which a high school teacher defended as having "a valid message" that describes a real world. "We are training youth now beyond just reading and writing," she said, prompting the opposition leader to respond: "We are not trying to censor anything. We are just trying to hold onto the moral values in America."
- *Dallas, Texas.* Peter Benchley's *Jaws*, Pete Gent's *North Dallas Forty*, and *Go Ask Alice* were taken off school library shelves after a school district review committee objected to their language—a move that prompted the executive director of the Classroom Teachers of Dallas, Herbert V. Cooke, Jr. to declare that the school district committee has "its head in the sand."
- *Roseburg, Oregon.* Taking note of a new Oregon obscenity law, a school official removed from the Roseburg High School library two dozen publications, including *The Catcher in the Rye* and a copy of *Time* magazine. "When in doubt, pull it off the shelf," he said.

- *Phoenix, Arizona.* "Do You Feel Bad After Sex?" An elementary school principal, spotting an article by this title in a copy of *Glamour* magazine on the library shelf, ordered the magazine removed, along with copies of *Time* and *Newsweek* that carried pictures of nude persons.

  "Go out and check your libraries," the principal told fellow school authorities. Citing nudity as inappropriate material for elementary school libraries, another principal said, "We certainly don't condone these magazines with this type of information."

- *Pinellas County, Florida.* Complaining of a "trend" toward the use of "filthy, godless works" in school classrooms and libraries, representatives of Churches United for Decency (CUD) and the Florida Action Committee for Education (FACE) carried their protest to the Florida Education Commissioner and to the Florida Senate Education Committee.

  One superintendent, replying to the book critics, said, "The panacea is to remove certain books – so drugs, racism, corruption in high levels of government will hereby not exist as far as the students are concerned. No group has the right to deny something they want to read."

- *South Portland, Maine.* Demanding the removal of D. W. Griffith's 1915 classic, *Birth of a Nation*, from the city library's fall film series, members of the National Association for the Advancement of

Colored People and the Association for Black Progress called the film "so negative in regards to the black contribution to the birth of the nation."

When the city agreed to drop the film, the *Portland Express* called the move an indication of a "readiness to bow to pressure and to engage in library censorship."

- *Oscoda, Michigan.* After the Oscoda Board of Education voted to remove *Rivers of Blood—Tears of Darkness,* a book about the Watts race riots, from the shelves of the high school library, a number of librarians protested in a letter to the board: "If an item is removed from the collection because of bad language, shouldn't all materials with bad language be removed? This would eliminate almost all new fiction, nonfiction, or magazines from the collection. . . . Other materials can and will be challenged. How much of a collection will you have? If an item is removed from the collection, what are you telling your children of their ability to read, reflect, and respond discriminately?"

- *Syracuse, Indiana.* In response to protests raised over a number of "cuss words" in John Steinbeck's *Of Mice and Men,* the book was removed from all required reading lists and from the school library.

- *Enid, Oklahoma.* After the mother of a junior high school student complained that certain passages in David Guammen's novel *To Walk the Line* were "unfit for junior high students to read," the board of education voted to ban the book from all libraries in the Enid public school system. The assistant superintendent explained about the difficulties of screening a great many books: "We don't try to justify the books that are found to be objectionable; we take them out of circulation immediately."

- *Englewood, Colorado.* After English teachers and librarians expressed their faith in the value of Pat Conroy's autobiographical *The Water is Wide,* the school board refused to ban the book from the city's schools, asserting that nonrequired reading can be controlled only when it affects particular children of parents. A junior high school student's father had raised the issue by objecting to the "irreverent use of God's name" and four-letter words in the book.

  In the same city, head librarian Harriet Lute of the Public Library denied a request made by a group of parents to remove from the library's shelves a collection of verse called *Beastly Boys and Ghastly Girls.* The librarian said that the book, which contains poems by Lewis Carroll, A. A. Milne, and others, is listed in many standard guides to children's literature. The parents had charged the book contained "out and out gore" and "needless violence."

- *Neillsville, Wisconsin.* Rejecting a plea that a parents group be allowed to censor books in the junior-senior high school library, the school board voted to permit the objectionable books to remain on the shelves. Among the titles: *The Grapes of Wrath, Of Mice and Men, Catch-22, Andersonville, The Catcher in the Rye, Soul on Ice*, and *The Fixer*.

What all of these controversies and conflicts add up to, it seems, is, as U.S. Commissioner of Education T. H. Bell has put it, "a growing concern on the part of parents that they have lost control over their children's education and, therefore, their children's future." But why *books* as targets? Because, as one explanation goes, the books, be they classroom texts or library volumes, are easily identifiable; they are very visible to concerned

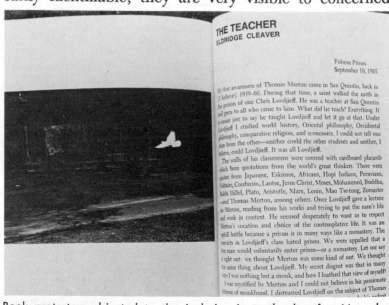

Book protesters objected to the inclusion in textbooks of writings by former Black Panther leader Eldridge Cleaver. *(William Tiernan)*

parents who see them as reflecting the shifting and hard-
to-cope-with new values of society.

A publisher explained: "Until a few years ago, publishers played it very safe. They were careful to exclude
material that might be objectionable to anyone, anywhere. That was Dullsville. Kids were turning off in
droves. The last few years, publishers have been trying
to find material that was more interesting, more hard
hitting, that the kids could relate to. They began to get
into subjects that would have been taboo a few years
ago."

But some parents say these books are more than just
hard hitting; they call them anti-Christian, anti-American, and just plain "dirty."

Take one of the books at the heart of the Neillsville,
Wisconsin, controversy—Black Panther leader Eldridge
Cleaver's *Soul on Ice*. In one objectionable excerpt, we
read:

> I became a rapist. To refine my technique and *modus
> operandi*, I started out by practicing on black girls
> in the ghetto . . . and when I considered myself
> smooth enough, I crossed the tracks and sought out
> white prey . . . Rape was an insurrectionary act.
> It delighted me that I was defying and trampling
> upon the white man's law, upon his system of val-
> ues, and that I was defiling his women . . .

Is this passage "dirty," anti-Christian, and anti-American?

There is no yes or no answer—the response will depend on your point of view—but let's look closer at another often objected to book, *The Catcher in the Rye*, which has been the object of hundreds of censorship attempts, making it probably the most widely censored book in America.

Here is how it begins:

> If you really want to hear about it, the first thing you'll probably want to know is where I was born, and what my lousy childhood was like, and how my parents were occupied and before they had me, and all that David Copperfield kind of crap, but I don't feel like going into it, if you want to know the truth. In the first place, that stuff bores me, and in the second place, my parents would have about two hemorrhages apiece if I told anything pretty personal about them. They're quite touchy about anything like that, especially my father. They're nice and all—I'm not saying that—but they're also touchy as hell. Besides, I'm not going to tell you my whole goddam autobiography or anything . . .

The story is told in the first person by a confused boy, Holden Caulfield, a prep-school runaway who goes around using four-letter words and making references to sexual experiences before he is finally confined to an institution. The language and the incidents, if taken separately, if viewed by themselves only, may indeed appear most shocking, may indeed appear "obscene."

But let's listen to an English professor, G. Robert Carlsen, of the University of Iowa, explain why *The Catcher in the Rye* is not an obscene book, but a work of literature. In his book *Books and the Teen-age Reader*, Carlsen says:

These details certainly have a lurid quality, and so a parent may feel that the book could be harmful for his adolescent son or daughter to read. But consider the second component of meaning—what does the author feel about the things that are happening to Holden? In other words what is the voice, the tonality, of the writer? What judgement towards Holden and the society he lives in is the author making? Salinger's attitude is one of great compassion for Holden and his confusion. He implies his own aching desire that life might be better and more meaningful to the boy. His tone is one of profound regret and grief that life must hold such torment and despair for a boy who wants a clean and beautiful world. Thus, the total impact of *The Catcher in the Rye* is something quite different from the individual incidents in the story. The author is not trying to shock the reader by a display of sex nor stir up lustful feelings in his young readers. He is honestly trying to picture the agonies a young person faces while growing up.

A convincing argument, perhaps. But would you want your *daughter* to read such a book, and such books as

God's Little Acre and *Sanctuary?* This is a question oft-posed by those who believe these books not fit for girls. Knowing that these books, by Erskine Caldwell and William Faulkner, contain numerous controversial passages, it might be difficult to answer the question. But as far back as 1949, in a widely publicized Pennsylvania case (*Commonwealth v. Gordon*), Judge Curtis Bok answered the question this way:

> It will be asked whether one would care to have one's young daughter read these books. I suppose that by the time she is old enough to wish to read them she will have learned the biologic facts of life and the words that go with them . . . I should prefer that my own three daughters meet the facts of life and the literature of the world in my library than behind a neighbor's barn, for I can face the adversary there directly. If the young ladies are appalled by what they read, they can close the book at the bottom of page one; if they read further, they will learn what is in the world and in its people, and no parents who have been discerning with their children need fear the outcome . . . Our daughters must live in the world and decide what sort of women they are to be, and we should be willing to prefer their deliberate and informed choice of decency rather than an innocence that continues to spring from ignorance.

"Things forbidden have a secret charm," said the Roman historian Tacitus.

So it is with books that shock. Because the ideas they express may be different, because the aspects of sex and love that they tell about may appear to glamorize or glorify the seamy side of life, they become immediately controversial—and the target of would-be "censors."

It is easy to see, therefore, why librarians are often at the heart of censorship controversies. Because the subject matter they handle is controversial, they themselves become controversial.

Before discussing in detail the plight of librarians, it is important to know that book-banning itself is nothing new. The Bible has been banned more than any other book in history. (It was first banned in 553 in Rome and most recently in 1956 in the Soviet Union.) Over the ages the works of Homer, Socrates, Confucius, Aristophenes, and Shakespeare have been banned. John Milton's *Paradise Lost* has been banned, and so have Mark Twain's *Huckleberry Finn* and *Tom Sawyer*, and, at one time or another thousands of other titles. Walt Whitman's *Leaves of Grass* shocked American puritanism and was banned in the nineteenth century. In 1939 Ernest Hemingway's *A Farewell to Arms* was attacked as "dirt." In 1939 Steinbeck's *The Grapes of Wrath* was banned, or burned, throughout America. Caldwell's *Tobacco Road* and *God's Little Acre* received much the same treatment. And many more of the best known works of America's most popular writers, including MacKinlay Kantor, James T. Farrell, John O'Hara, Norman Mailer, and James Baldwin, all have gone through the censorship wringer. Even *Jack and the Beanstalk* has felt the sting of censorship—for supposedly teaching children to

Censored American classics. At one time or another, each of these books has been subjected to censorship attempts. *(Gerald S. Snyder)*

lie and steal. *Mickey Mouse,* the internationally syndicated comic strip, has also run into censorship troubles—once (in 1932 in the United States) because the strip showed a cow resting in a pasture reading Elinor Glyn's *Three Weeks,* a novel held to contain "improper" language.

In the following list of books and magazines, which at one time or another have been either censored or condemned, the judgments characteristic of would-be censors are cited by the National Council of Teachers of English (NCTE):

- Plato's *Republic:* "This book is un-Christian."
- George Eliot's *Silas Marner:* "You can't prove what that dirty old man is doing with that child between chapters."
- Jules Verne's *Around the World in Eighty Days:* "Very unfavorable to Mormons."
- Nathaniel Hawthorne's *The Scarlet Letter:* "A filthy book."
- Shakespeare's *Macbeth:* "Too violent for children today."
- Fyodor Dostoyevsky's *Crime and Punishment:* "Serves as a poor model for young people."
- Herman Melville's *Moby Dick:* "Contains homosexuality."
- J. D. Salinger's *Catcher in the Rye:* "A dreadful dreary recital of sickness, sordidness, and sadism."
- Kurt Vonnegut's *Slaughterhouse-Five:* "Its repetitious obscenity and immorality merely degrade and defile, teaching nothing."

- Edward Albee's *Zoo Story:* "Pure filth."
- Harper Lee's *To Kill a Mockingbird:* "The word raped is used several times. Children should not see this in any literature book."
- Ralph Ellison's *Invisible Man:* "The book is biased on the black question."
- Anne Frank's *Diary of a Young Girl:* "Obscene and blasphemous."
- Eldridge Cleaver's *Soul on Ice:* "Totally objectionable and without any literature value."
- Warren Miller's *The Cool World:* "Why do kids have to read books like that?"
- *National Geographic:* "Nudity and sensationalism, especially in stories on barbaric foreign people."
- *Scholastic Magazine:* "Doctrines opposing the beliefs of the majority, socialistic programs; promotes racial unrest and contains very detailed geography of foreign countries, especially those inhabited by dark people."
- *National Observer:* "Right-wing trash with badly reported news."
- *The New York Times:* "That thing should be outlawed after printing the Pentagon papers and helping our country's enemies."

Concludes the NCTE: "We can safely make two statements about censorship: first, any work is potentially open to attack by someone, somewhere, sometime, for some reason; second, censorship is often arbitrary and irrational."

Understanding further the reasons for library troubles with censors, we see that race relations frequently form the reason for attacks on librarians.

In 1941, for example, Governor Eugene Talmadge of Georgia ordered that any books that offended the South, the Bible, or Georgia be banned from college and school libraries.

In 1950, in Bartlesville, Oklahoma, a librarian with thirty-one years of service was fired because she displayed in her library certain magazines which a Citizens' Committee considered undesirable, and because the librarian had taken part in community race relations discussions. (In 1952, the Oklahoma Supreme Court voted for this librarian and against the City Commission which had taken control of the library.)

In 1959, the idea of interracial cooperation and pro-integration points of view prompted the Georgia Board of Education to order that its literary committee give its stamp of approval on all library books. The same year a children's book called *The Rabbits' Wedding*, showing a marriage ceremony between a black rabbit and a white rabbit, was forced to the "reserved" shelf of the Alabama Public Library Service Division after a charge by the Alabama State Senate that it was really an appeal for racial integration.

When race relations is not the issue, the "language" of books usually is. To take just one example of this, consider that in 1963 Max Rafferty, the California Superintendent of Public Instruction, called for a "little bit of censorship" to ban from school libraries *A Dictionary of American Slang*, which Rafferty's supporters claimed was "dirty." They cited 150 questionable words from the more than 8,000 in the book. In one city the book was burned; in many others it was ordered off the library shelves, or put on restricted shelf lists.

In numerous other cases through the years, librarians have fought off the censors—or been hounded by them.

In a few early rare occasions, librarians themselves had a hand in book censorship. In 1876, for instance, *The Adventures of Tom Sawyer* was banned from the Brooklyn (New York) Public Library as "unsuitable" for young people; in 1885 *The Adventures of Huckleberry Finn* got the same treatment from the Public Library in Concord, Massachusetts (the hometown of Henry David Thoreau); and in 1905 both of these Mark Twain books were criticized by the Brooklyn Public Library as setting bad examples for young people.

(With tongue in cheek, Mark Twain replied to his critics: "I am greatly troubled by what you say. I wrote *Tom Sawyer* and *Huck Finn* for adults exclusively, and it always distresses me when I find that boys and girls have been allowed access to them. The mind that becomes soiled in youth can never again be washed clean.")

In self-defense, librarians declare that they cannot choose only "clean" books, for to do this—even if they did know for sure what constitutes "clean"—would be to ignore a great deal of what is current, relevant, artistic, or intellectually important. As one librarian put it: "This kind of selection, weeding out the 'unclean,' would be to place the librarian in the role of censor."

It is wrong, too, the librarians assert, that just because they are librarians they have the right to decide what individuals should or should not read. "It is unreasonable to expect me to read and put my stamp of approval on every book in my library," said the same librarian.

More formally put, in a joint statement of the American Library Association and the Association of American Publishers:

> There is no place in our society for efforts to coerce the taste of others, to confine adults to the reading matter deemed suitable for adolescents, or to inhibit the efforts of writers to achieve artistic expression. To some, much of modern literature is shocking. But is not much of life itself shocking? We cut off literature at the source if we prevent writers from dealing with the stuff of life . . .
>
> In a free society each individual is free to determine for himself what he wishes to read, and each group is free to determine what it will recommend to its freely associated members. But no group has the right to take the law into its own hands, and to impose its own concept of politics or morality upon other members of a democratic society. Freedom is no freedom if it is accorded only to the accepted and the inoffensive.

The librarians who so often are out there defending the use of words frequently are caught up in their meaning. In California, for instance, librarians faced a

jail term under a 1969 law that said they had to withhold "harmful matter" from minors. The problem: What
constitutes "harmful matter?" Who is to make this decision? When a Los Angeles Superior Court struck down
the "harmful matter" provision from the state law, the
Sacramento Bee called the decision "a victory for reason
and common sense, and for the freedom of libraries to
serve their ultimate purpose—the wide dissemination of
knowledge and information."

The civil action against this law was funded by the
Freedom to Read Foundation, the legal arm of the
35,000-member American Library Association, the oldest
library association in the world (founded in 1876) which
interprets the First Amendment as applying to libraries
as "the responsibility of the library to provide books
and other materials presenting all points of view concerning the problems and issues of our times." According to the ALA's *Library Bill of Rights,* no library materials should be proscribed or removed because of
partisan or doctrinal disapproval, and the right of an individual to the use of the library should not be denied
or abridged because of age, race, religion, national
origin, or social or political views.

To deny the rights of individuals the freedom to read
what they wish is censorship, in the ALA's view. Yet
it is important not to misuse the word "censorship." It
is important to approach it carefully, weighing its context and its implications. For it can be, and often is, a
loaded word, with many different shades of meaning, a
word that is often misused. The charge of "censorship"
becomes propaganda, for instance, when a certain book

Library Bill of Rights

The Council of the American Library Association reaffirms its belief in the following basic policies which should govern the services of all libraries.

1. As a responsibility of library service, books and other library materials selected should be chosen for values of interest, information and enlightenment of all the people of the community. In no case should library materials be excluded because of the race or nationality or the social, political, or religious views of the authors.

2. Libraries should provide books and other materials presenting all points of view concerning the problems and issues of our times; no library materials should be proscribed or removed from libraries because of partisan or doctrinal disapproval.

3. Censorship should be challenged by libraries in the maintenance of their responsibility to provide public information and enlightenment.

4. Libraries should cooperate with all persons and groups concerned with resisting abridgment of free expression and free access to ideas.

5. The rights of an individual to the use of a library should not be denied or abridged because of his age, race, religion, national origins or social or political views.

6. As an institution of education for democratic living, the library should welcome the use of its meeting rooms for socially useful and cultural activities and discussion of current public questions. Such meeting places should be available on equal terms to all groups in the community regardless of the beliefs and affiliations of their members, provided that the meetings be open to the public.

Adopted June 18, 1948.
Amended February 2, 1961, and June 27, 1967, by the ALA Council.

"Censorship should be challenged," asserts the American Library Association. *(American Library Association)* is chosen by a library's book selection committee, and another is not. It is not correct to label this censorship, because it is vital that some books be selected and others rejected—the book was not banned, or "censored"—it simply was not chosen. In its more critical definition, censorship, as generally referred to in this book, means the deliberate attempt to suppress ideas—to ban a book or a movie or a newspaper story or anything else that attempts to convey an idea.

Then what in libraries may properly be called censorship? There is no simple answer to this question, but there are certain guidelines to help determine the difference between censorship and selection.

The librarian must make a decision. She (or he) cannot pick every title she hears or reads about; there would not be money enough to buy them all, not shelves enough to stock them even if she could buy them. So she decides to buy some books and not to buy others. In its purest form, selection was operative, not censorship, not any attempt at suppression. As the ALA points out: "Libraries do not advocate the ideas found in their collections. The presence of a magazine or book in a library does not indicate an endorsement of its contents by the library."

What if the librarian attempts to foist her tastes upon the library's users? That indeed may be a form of censorship. For what one librarian may find "objectionable," another may find quite "acceptable." In the words of a librarian concerned with the problem: "The real question of censorship versus selection arises when the librarian, exercising his own judgment, decides against a book which has every legal right to representation on his shelves. In other words, we should not have been concerned with the librarian who refused to buy *Ulysses* for his library before 1933, but we do have an interest in his refusal after the courts cleared it for general circulation in the United States."

Since we've brought up the subject of *Ulysses* (this James Joyce classic was once banned by the United States Post Office Department), suppose a pressure group of one type or another exerted its influence to get it removed from a library. The group may have claimed selection, not censorship, but a very strong case could be made for calling it an act of censorship. The librarian, remember, said, "I will not circulate this book," or "This library will not circulate this book." The pressure group, however, said, "This book must not be circulated, not in this library, not in this community." The group may represent only a small segment of the community, but by its action it tried to force its will against *Ulysses* upon the entire community—and that is censorship.

Most important, the *motives* of the selector/censor are what really matter. There is, in other words, quite a difference between the librarian who turns down a certain book because the library had insufficient funds to pay for it and the pressure group who tried to keep the same book out of the library because it espoused an unpopular idea. In the first instance, the librarian was selecting; in the second, the pressure group was censoring. The end result may be the same—the book stays out of the library—but the *intent* is very different.

Other elements to be considered in deciding whether censorship is or is not occurring may deal with the intent of the *writer*. Was the writer's intent pornographic or artistic? This may be extremely difficult to decide, for some of the great works of literature, such as *Ulysses*, have been out of step with their time—so new in their approach as to shock or to make the reader feel that perhaps the intent was indeed pornographic, when it was artistic all along.

In trying to form a way for determining the all-important difference between selection and censorship, one librarian notes that the selector's approach usually is positive, the rejector's negative. "To the selector, the important thing is to find reasons to take the book." But the censor looks for "reasons to reject the book; his guiding principle leads him to seek out the objectionable features, the weaknesses, the possibilities for misinterpretation."

"The selector says, if there is anything good in this book let us try to keep it; the censor says, if there is anything bad in this book, let us reject it."

Applying this standard, the citizens in the tiny New Hampshire mill community of Hillsborough, who in 1975 signed a petition objecting to "taxpayers' money being used to buy obscene books and books with obscene language in them," would be deemed censors, and not selectors. They sought to reject the books for the "bad" they contained. They were seeking out the objectionable; they did not look for the values, the strengths, the virtues, in the books.

The "censor" label is one that nobody wants. As one

of the Hillsborough citizens declared: "They say it's censorship, but if movies can be rated R and X, and if that isn't censorship, why is this considered to be?"

Sometimes out of deep conviction a group unwarily gets into the role of censor, and then learns that it is censoring and renounces that role. A recent interesting case concerned the Church of Scientology. Dropping a libel suit it had brought against public libraries in Hamilton and Etobicoke, Canada, to prevent the circulation of *The Scandal of Scientology, Inside Scientology, Scientology: The New Religion,* and *The Mind Benders,* a spokesman for the Church told the Canadian Library Association: "We have concluded that our interests are parallel . . . We agree that the libraries should be free to circulate literature in the public interest of free speech and that intellectual freedom, a basic tenet of our creed, must be upheld."

The single most vicious example of censorship occurred not in America, but in Germany, when on May 10, 1933, on the Franz Joseph Platz between the University of Berlin and the State Opera on Unter den Linden, the contents of public and private libraries were tossed into a pyre. While students performed Indian dances and the flames soared, the works of authors who displeased the Nazis went up in flames.

Later, in the 1930s, while signing a proclamation reducing postage rates on books, President Franklin D. Roosevelt sounded a rallying cry for the right to read when he said: "Here is the difference between Nazism and Democracy. They are burning books, while we here are going to make them as available as possible."

4

Television: Censoring Violence

One Sunday night in 1974, in the parking lot of a fundamentalist church in Battle Creek, Michigan, hundreds of aroused parishioners gathered to show their resentment of "sinful" television programming by tossing into a bonfire eleven television sets worth about $1,400. Before throwing his set into the flames, one church member blew out the picture tube with a shotgun. Another declared: "The programs are poisoning our children's minds. I had to censor everything my sons watched. Even on one of my favorite shows, the 'Mary Tyler Moore Show,' they used swear words. The last show I heard the word 'damn.'"

Other citizens, while not so angered as to burn their sets, and not as offended by just the word "damn," are, however, equally disturbed. "Why are decent citizens not up in arms against the filth brought into our homes by the TV set?" asked a Virginia woman in a letter of protest to a local newspaper. "Children are being educated in the ways of prostitutes and pimps, of callgirls and go-go dancers. I refer to scatalogical innuendos and acrobatics, to couples perpetually going to bed suggestively, to vulgarities that are not merely tasteless, they are foul. Depravity·is a dead end. Quickly we become, as the Spaniards say, *gastado,* spent. And then there is nowhere left to go."

An Iowa couple wrote to Senator John O. Pastore (Dem.) of Rhode Island, chairman of the Senate's Communications Subcommittee: "Please do all you can to clean up the screen—the crime, violence, sex, and all. We believe [the violence] has a great influence on children and young adults, and this is why there is such an increase in bad behavior among them."

Another Congressman, Torbert H. Macdonald, recently said on the subject of TV violence: "The bloodshed and killing in shows like 'S.W.A.T.' is the worst thing to hit the United States since the plague."

Many people, among them many respected psychologists, would agree, maintaining that television brutality can influence children to do wrong. There are a few documented cases. It has been claimed, for instance, that a television movie showing a group of teenagers pouring gasoline over a derelict and setting him afire actually inspired someone to do the same to a woman in Boston who died from the flames. After watching a rock star conduct a mock hanging on television, one youth tried the same—and died. In Los Angeles, police asked one network to set up a special screening of a television program they believed might have inspired a killer to slash the throats of three skid row derelicts; the same kind of crime had been featured on the program. And charging that a rape scene on one TV film stimulated a similar attack on her daughter, a California woman sued the producers of the film.

This cause-effect relationship means, if it is true, that television actually can teach children to be antisocial, unnaturally aggressive, or even violent. "In too many TV films, we see a glorification of violence that makes heroes of killers," as one critic of TV violence put it. "The primary motivation for all of this is money and the fierce scramble for ratings."

There is no question that there is plenty of violence to be seen on television. In a television "violence profile" compiled at the Annenberg School of Communications at the University of Pennsylvania, it was found that nearly three-fourths of all programs in the 1973-74 tele-

Television violence—an issue central to the discussion of television censorship. *(Garry Trudeau and Action for Children's Television)*

vision season contained violence of one type or another. United States Congressman John M. Murphy of New York, who conducted a study into the frequency of violent episodes on television, found that on one of the three major networks, 71 percent of the prime-time shows were loaded with violent sequences, while the other networks followed close behind with 67 and 57 percent of their major shows portraying violence.

It is estimated that each year the average American youngster between the ages of 5 and 15 views 13,000 killings on the tube, because in almost all American homes—some 96 percent—there is at least one television set, and this set is on about six hours per day. It is a fact that school-age children spend more time in front of the television set than they do in front of teachers; the average 16-year-old spends some 14,000 hours at the TV set—4,000 hours more than spent in the classroom.

Parents fear that the depiction of violence will "rub off" onto their children. Yet the argument that television violence breeds actual violence—an argument central to the discussion of television censorship—never has been resolved. Despite the fact that America has been called "an armed camp" because of the 40 million handguns in circulation—accounting for an estimated 10,000 murders, 13,000 suicides, and 90,000 armed assaults each year—no "causal" relationship has been shown to connect television films or shows and these statistics.

This is not to say that there is *no* causal relationship. Indeed, in 1972 a committee appointed by the Surgeon General of the United States to study the problem de-

cided that: "There is an indication of causal relation
between viewing televised violence and aggressive behavior in children."

The point is, however, that the committee could not
decide which children are likely to be affected or how
many or for how long or to what extent. This lead three
eminent men in the field of communication theory,
Wilbur Schramm, Jack Lyle, and Edwin Parker, to comment: "For *some* children, under *some* conditions, some
television is harmful. For other children under the same
conditions, or for the same children under *other* conditions, it may be beneficial. For *most* children, under
most conditions, *most* television is probably neither particularly harmful nor particularly beneficial." (Emphasis
in original text.)

In other words, no one really knows very much about
the effect on children (or adults) of seeing violence
played out.

A number of years ago, for example, a teenager mur-
dered his date after viewing a movie. *Anatomy of a
Murder?* Not at all. The film was Walt Disney's *Snow
White and the Seven Dwarfs.*

The two points of view, so jarringly different from
each other go something like this:

Seeing violence stimulates children aggressively; it
also shows them how to commit aggressive acts.

*   *   *

Violence depicted on the home screen will continue to have almost no effect on the behavior of man, woman or child except for the occasional hero who heaves the set out the window.

As the continuing controversy about violence on television mounts, and as more and more people demand that the television industry do something about TV violence, it is easy to see how the emotional issue of censorship arises. Since the First Amendment guarantees freedom of speech, it is the legitimate right of the broadcast media to resist any attempt to restrict this freedom.

The television critics are quick to respond that they are not trying to censor television, but to change it. Yet it is difficult to deny that they are practicing, or advocating, at least a form of censorship.

There always has been some form of television censorship. Even since the very first shows, sponsors have been having their say—"suppressing parts deemed objectionable"—about what is or is not shown on the tube. They reviewed scripts and otherwise held firm control over shows—particularly when it came to sex. In the early days of television this sometimes went to extremes. In all of the "Superman" shows from 1953 to 1957, for instance, Lois Lane, star reporter for the Daily Planet, who had a crush on Mr. Mighty, never once kissed him. The show's sponsor wouldn't like it, recently explained Noel Neill, the first actress to play Lois, who once was dropped from a proposed commercial featuring the show's main characters, because, she said, the sponsor thought it would "just be wrong for us to be sitting at a table eating breakfast together."

About this time also, the kind of language used on television was watched very closely. Words like "pimp," "pregnant," "rape," "virgin"—even words like "damn" and "hell"—would have been censored.

Today, there can be no doubt, television has come a long way in adapting to contemporary mores. Now all of the above words are used, and more, even "God damn" and "son of a bitch," although it should be noted right here that expressions like these last two are allowed only on rare occasions, when network officials deem the words essential to honestly portray a character. In the case of the last two expressions, they were permitted to be spoken by actor James Whitmore on a CBS "60 Minutes" program because the actor was impersonating the rough-talking former president, Harry S Truman— and that is how Harry Truman spoke. Used in a different context, the words might very well have been judged indecent, and the network officials would have censored them. But in the case of Harry Truman, it was viewed they were necessary to capture the real flavor of the man.

The television censors (found in departments of "standards and practices") are always careful to check for street language vocabulary. On taped programs there is no problem to see what is coming, but on live broadcasts they use an electronic delay device that allows them to see or hear, seconds before the audience does, all material that goes over the air, so that words can quickly be deleted before it is "too late."

Some of the biggest stars on television have experienced difficulties with the network censors. When, for example, in a ninety-minute special, Cher Bono and Bette Midler took the role of prostitutes in a musical number called "Trash Ladies," the censors felt they "really looked like hookers," and objected strenuously.

Comedian Richard Pryor, among others, has had troubles because of the street language "authenticity" of his monologues, with words deleted ("Pryor Restraint," someone called it) because, said the censors, they did not fit within "the general realm of acceptable late-night television vocabulary."

Of course it is not just what people say that offends the censors, but the way people look. In one instance, the censors objected to the scanty costumes worn by Cher and her guest Raquel Welch. They were doing a duet and the problem was that it simply showed too much of Cher and Raquel; they looked "too sexy." The censors ordered the skit restaged, which spurred an argument over who was to foot the enormous cost of the restaging.

There is plenty of network censorship over the use of words especially, and plenty of dislike for it. Television personality Dick Cavett on the subject, for instance: "I have found TV censorship to be so petty, niggling, small-minded and silly that it is well-nigh impossible to wax eloquent on the subject. It would be an imposition to disturb the ghosts of Voltaire, Milton or Zenger when the issue at hand is usually something like whether a starlet's use of the word 'bastard' will have to be snipped out of a program to protect America from God (if even He knows what)."

At the present it is a crime to use "indecent" language

on the air. But the trouble of course is that what may appear to be indecent one year may not appear so the next, and what is indecent to one person or group of persons may be quite acceptable to others. In other words, people's standards and views change, depending on the mores of society.

Meanwhile, the business of deciding which words to allow and which to disallow poses a very serious problem for the broadcast industry. Not wanting to deny freedom of speech, and also not wishing to be offensive, they must judge each case on its own merits and, more often than not, they will settle for the middle ground. While abhoring the idea of censorship, they must make a judgment—one that may be correct or incorrect, depending on whose opinion you go by—but a judgment nevertheless.

In the case of television violence, the judgment to censor or not to censor constantly runs into greater difficulty, because television programming is composed of shows of numerous types and categories. There is no single set of standards for all shows, no way to draw a clear distinction between suitable and unsuitable, and no way to make sure that certain standards for programs are enforced. The television networks are not licensed, and the companies that produce and distribute the shows for the networks are free to use their own discretion about the kind of shows they think should be shown.

One government agency, the Federal Communications Commission (FCC), does have licensing authority over the stations that carry the programs sent out by the networks; but Congress prohibits the seven-member FCC from interfering with the content of programs or from taking any action which smacks of censorship.

The FCC, as a government agency, is uncertain about its authority. "Any rule-making in these areas," it has said, "would require finding an appropriate balance between the need to protect children from harmful material and the adult audience's interest in diverse programming. Government rules could create the risk of improper governmental interference in sensitive, subjective decisions about programming, could tend to freeze present standards and could also discourage creative developments in the medium." Yet the FCC has been urged by Congress to take some move that would guard children against the continuing wave of violent and possibly obscene material being shown on television. This action came after thousands of citizens wrote letters of complaint to the Commission about certain shows. The protest wave turned into an avalanche. In 1972, the FCC received about 2,000 complaints about violent or sexually-oriented programs. In 1974, the number of complaints zoomed to almost 25,000, and the letters (many the result of organized letter-writing campaigns) show no signs of stopping.

Television stations too, in a most unusual action, began urging the FCC to do something about changing the network programming of adult shows; the networks, they complained, did not notify them about potentially offensive or controversial shows, and so there was no time to warn viewers.

In the mid-1970s, as criticism over television violence

mounted, the networks began to preface certain "adult"
and more "mature" shows with a warning: "We suggest
you consider whether the program should be viewed
by young people or others in your home who might be
disturbed by it."

The idea was that children need to be protected from
adult television programs that depict violent, obscene,
or indecent scenes.

It was a noble intention, but one that constantly ran
into trouble, for it was found that if viewers were
warned, giving more publicity to the potentially objectionable programs, this only created interest—and many
of those shows got the highest ratings. The networks
suggested that parents, not television executives, decide
what programs their children should or should not watch.

"Basically, networks produce the kinds of programs
that the audience demonstrates it likes," says ratings
expert Herb Jacobs, president of TelCom. "If the public
wants police stories and Westerns, it's pretty hard to
dramatize them without some violence. The situation
comedies have gotten away from slapstick and are moving toward more real-life subjects, and viewers are lov-
ing it."

Apparently the truth is that violence incites interest,
and interest means viewers, and viewers mean that the
sponsors products are going to be bought. It is the
market, therefore, that determines what kinds of shows
are produced, and this generally means that people get
the kind of shows they want; since unpopular shows do
not stay on the air long, they have little chance to sell

the sponsor's product. And since the sponsor does want to sell his product, he wishes to give viewers what will most appeal to them.

The idea that television basically gives people what they want was further emphasized by an official of the National Academy of Television Arts and Sciences, who said: "Violence and sex on TV is a serious question that people in the industry should be concerned about and should resolve by taking the more outrageous and titillating scenes off the air. But this is also a good political issue in Washington, and sometimes people in Congress are a little hypocritical when they say the public deserves better programs. Basically, networks give the public what the public wants."

It is also argued that television shows the world as it is, that it is a mere "mirror" of society, reflecting not only the activities of society, but its changing attitudes, particularly those that bear on such headline issues as race, sexuality, and human relationships. It follows, therefore, as this theory goes, that television is no better or worse than the society it mirrors.

In referring to the presentation of mature themes on television, Herbert S. Schlosser, president of NBC has said that one of the broadcaster's prime responsibilities is "to balance a respect for creative freedom with an equal respect for the sensitivities of an audience with a wide diversity of tastes and interests." He says, "We must serve the millions of viewers who want at least part of their entertainment to relate to experience of the world with which they can identify. In keeping pace with the times, we do not intend to leap too far ahead of what viewers will accept, but we cannot lag so far behind that they leave us and turn elsewhere."

Critics of network program selection often point to the broader responsibilities of television to provide programs of high quality and real social value.

Chief Judge David L. Bazelon of the U.S. Court of Appeals for the District of Columbia, which hears all appeals from licensing decisions of the FCC, puts it this way: "The broadcast media must strongly resist all government attempts to interfere with their legitimate discretion. But on the other hand, they must also have the strength to admit their shortcomings, their abuse of the immense power of television for the private profit of a few, to the serious detriment of the nation at large . . . The broadcast media know—or should know—when their programming is simply and only mass appeal pablum designed to titillate a sufficiently large majority to enable the broadcasters to sell the most advertising . . . They know the impact of their programs on children, they know about the marketing of human emotions and of the prurient interest in violence and sex."

Perhaps the would-be "censors" have a point. Perhaps all of the violence seen on television is not really necessary. Perhaps, as the network critics contend, the popularity of such shows as *All in the Family*, *Sandford & Son*, *The Waltons*, and *I Love Lucy*, prove that long runs are possible without succumbing to the temptation to use scenes of violence.

Of late, more and more people are casting aside the charge of censorship and demanding that television change. Two women who did this, Evelyn Kaye Sarson and Peggy Charren, in 1968 began to research television programming in an effort to see what could be done, and found that every television executive they spoke to referred to the "two-to-eleven-year-old market." Tired of commercialism, they founded Action for Children's Television (ACT), which went on to become a national organization, funded by the Ford and John and Mary R. Markle foundations and the Carnegie Corporation of New York, with the purpose of reforming children's programming.

"We were concerned about violence," said Mrs. Charren, "but also with the values portrayed and with the lack of diversity. We couldn't say that one lousy program would ruin a child for life. But a steady diet of supermen, batmen, and ghost chasers—those had to be at least a distortion of the world."

Not to confuse change with censorship, Mrs. Charren explained: "The problem for us was how to make change. We didn't think a boycott of sponsors would work . . . and we don't believe in censorship. The most obvious tactic was to create a climate of opinion that would pressure the broadcasters. So we went into the consciousness-raising business."

To "raise consciousness," ACT campaigned from its offices in Newtonville, Massachusetts, for an end to commercials on children's programs—a controversial campaign that prompted FCC chairman Richard E. Wiley to remark (at an advertising industry luncheon): "I am convinced that an elimination of advertising is not the answer to improving children's programming. On the contrary, it is my view that advertising support for such fare must be encouraged if adequate budgets are to be committed to the task of producing quality programming."

Replies ACT: funding for these programs must come from sources other than advertising revenues. The commercials must go, or change, because they foist super-sugary foods on children, and force children to pressure their parents to buy. As one speaker put it at an ACT symposium: "Commercialism bombards us all and all too frequently with messages which say you have to have something besides yourself to get along. You have to have a pill for a headache or smoke to feel cool or a drink to cope or, worst of all, a toy to play [with]. Your resources are not enough, so be sure to buy ours. Our children are being raised on messages like this, and what is more, they think we adults condone them."

Some people call ACT a censorship group, particularly television industry spokesmen who have accused ACT of trying to infringe on the constitutional rights of advertisers who claim a right to promote their products and services directly to children.

ACT disagrees, asserting that it is not censorship that the group advocates, but simply a raising of standards of television broadcasting and a lessening of the emphasis on advertising. Censorship, ACT contends, implies pressure for regulation of program content, and ACT asks only for regulations to govern the conditions under which programs are made. It wants to change the commercial system, not change particular programs, leaving that up to the broadcasters.

"The First Amendment," ACT says, "does not prohibit reasonable restrictions on advertising. ACT seeks only to secure the rights of children to be safe and healthy, and to protect their freedom to learn how to make responsible choices and decisions, based on an unclouded presentation of information."

In response to the pressures exerted by ACT and other groups, change is coming about. The networks are more closely eyeing the quality of children's television, some guidelines have been established for commercials pitched to children, and in early 1975, in response to a national clamor that violence on the tube be toned down, the FCC announced it would ask Congress to adopt legislation that would ban "the visual depiction of obscene or indecent material" on the air.

The FCC can only propose. But FCC Commissioner Glen O. Robinson also called for a "limited regulation" of offensive speech. He said: "It seems to be legitimate that there be a limited regulation of offensive speech which is purveyed widely, publicly, and indiscriminately in such a manner that it cannot be avoided without significantly inconveniencing people or infringing on their right to choose what they will see and hear."

Generally, network and station executives feel that the so-called "adult" shows should be shown during hours when most children are asleep. This might work except for the fact that children go to sleep at different hours, and even if they didn't, the different time zones throughout the United States would interfere. A 10 P.M. program, in the Eastern time zone, for instance, would be carried at 9 P.M. in the Central time zone, at

8 P.M. in the Mountain time zone, and at 7 P.M. in the Pacific time zone.

It is easy to see, therefore, that a curfew for adult programs would be impractical. "The entire system would have to rearrange itself," noted one television critic, "sending programs out separately so that all parts of the country played the same programs at the same hour regardless of time zones." Even if these were "clean" viewing stretches, what is to say that the networks might not cram more sex and violence shows into the other time slots?

The networks are trying, however. When, for example, NBC-TV found that it had scheduled a movie called "Death Stalk" after a program named "Winnie the Pooh and the Blustery Day," it feared that children might stay around and catch some of the violence, so it substituted for the film one called "Punch and Jody." Generally also, more adult-type shows are being scheduled during evening "family viewing" times—but not wholly without controversy.

"Family viewing" is a form of censorship, contend many creative producers and writers, who see it as a direct assault on program content, a "conspiracy" to violate the First Amendment.

What is suitable for "family viewing?" No one knows for sure, but the general understanding in the industry is that this excludes programs showing excessive violence, candid sexuality, or any other subject matter considered too inappropriate for children.

It seems fairly safe to say that there can never be

absolute assurance that children will be protected from "objectionable" material. As for the young people themselves, many don't seem to like the idea of having their programs censored, regardless of the form this censorship takes.

"I'm sick and tired of being run out of the family room because there's something on the TV that's not for little kids," wrote an eleven-year-older to the FCC.

Another youngster, writing to a television magazine, complained about "all those ridiculous, overprotective parents" who plan what their children will watch. "I am 13 and my parents let me watch what I like. They are not weird or funny by doing this. They know I know about sex. Besides some of these shows are good comedy shows. These aren't grandma's days when everyone thought babies were found in dead tree stumps. This is 1975."

One newspaper, commenting on the storm of protests, editorialized that "human beings have an extraordinarily wide range of tastes and one man's leavings may well be another's marinade." Observed the editorial writer: the greatest problem lies with the parents, not the programs.

"'My wife has to keep shooing the children out of the room,' a colleague of ours confided the other day," said the writer.

"'Why don't you just switch channels?' someone asked.

"'Because I'm watching it,' was the reply."

5

Movies: Art or Pornography?

In *Gone With the Wind,* Margaret Mitchell's classic story about the Civil War, there is a memorable scene at the end when Rhett Butler finally turns to his wife, Scarlett O'Hara, and announces in disgust that he is leaving her, whereupon she pleads with him, asks what she will do, and Rhett looks her straight in the eye and proclaims: "Frankly, my dear, I don't care."

At least, that is the way it *would* have been had the censor of the famous movie had his way, for the real line used by Rhett, and the one from the book, "Frankly, my dear, I don't give a damn," was held in 1939 to be sheer profanity: only people of the worst sort used words like that!

It was only after the pleading of the producer, David O. Selznick, that the offending word was allowed; yet some other things did end up on the cutting room floor—lines like: "May your mean little soul burn in hell for eternity," from Rhett to Scarlett; "I've never held fidelity to be a virtue" and "He can't be faithful to his wife with his mind, or unfaithful with his body," (more lines by Rhett). Even the innocent uttering of Dilcey; "An' whut it takes to feed a hungry chil' ah got," was cut by the censor—for reasons no one is quite certain of.

But all of this happened of course in a time when the censor reigned over Hollywood, when motion pictures that were not completely inoffensive did not receive the industry's seal of approval and so could not be shown without problems. In those days, if a man was shown embracing a woman on a bed, he had to have two feet on the floor; and not until the 1960s was it permitted to show the female navel (a jewel was often used as a cover-up).

Today all of this is changed. Almost every word imaginable is permitted, the worst forms of violence are depicted, and no subject—from homosexuality to rape, adultery to dope addiction—is taboo. Moviemakers are free to film whatever scenes they wish, the only restrictions being the limits of good taste or, more accurately, the morals and mores which the public will allow.

Movies have been termed "barometers of national mores," and, to use an understatement of understatements, "times have changed."

As Murray Schumach puts it in his book on movie and television censorship, *The Face on the Cutting Room Floor*, "One can, by studying the exposure of the female anatomy in films of different periods, almost calibrate the attitudes of the average man and woman in the United States toward sex, obscenity, vulgarity, pornography." As people become less puritanical, as they

Censors of the classic "Gone With the Wind" objected to Clark Gable's use of the *word* "damn." (*Museum of Modern Art/Film Stills Archive*)

become less offended by scenes showing the naked human body, the moviemakers are quick to sense this, and it is not boldness but rather a desire to be "with the times" that prompts them to put on film what years ago would have been considered sacrilegious or downright obscene.

Today there is an official censorship board in only one state (Maryland). The Catholic Church's Legion of Decency, formed in 1934 to advise Catholics about objectionable films, has been disbanded for years, after decades of putting pressure on the movie industry to improve the moral quality of films—by putting its "C" or "Condemned" ratings on them. So favorable generally is the climate today that there is no censorship *before* a thing is produced or made public—no *prior restraint*— or suppression of any kind on movies.

This is not to say that attempts at censorship have not been made. For years many states have been trying to get laws adopted that would restrict certain movies from the theaters. In 1974 alone, some 350 pieces of obscenity legislation directed against motion pictures were introduced in state legislatures. The Motion Picture Association of America (MPAA) fought the proposed legislation, and to date there is not a single state law prohibiting certain types of movies from being shown.

While a few cities do have censorship groups, the national rule is that any form of movie may be shown, the movie industry relying on a voluntary self-regulation rating system (G for general public, PG for parental guidance suggested, R for restricted to persons over seventeen, and X for movies of questionable nature). Only in the case of R and X-rated films are minors actually prohibited from seeing movies. Motion picture industry executives fear that unless they use such a rating system, the states might move in and rate—or try to censor—movies.

Censorship of movies, as we shall see, is not entirely a thing of the past, but to gain some insight into how exactly American mores have changed over the years, weakening many attempts at censorship, it is helpful to look at a number of film classics which had trouble with the censors, and see why they were censored. Many of these movies are being shown today—in art theaters, as reruns in local movie houses, and on television:

- *Battleground* (1949): In a scene about the Battle of the Bulge, German planes dropped leaflets over an isolated American squadron. A soldier picked a leaflet up, and when his buddy asked him what he was going to do with it, the soldier replied "Guess." The censors disallowed this and a new segment was shot showing the soldier picking up the leaflet and walking off without saying anything.
- *The Outlaw* (1946): In a film said to mark the beginning of Hollywood's "mammary madness," so much furor was created over the overexposed Jane Russell's bosom that the censors protested the "inescapable suggestion of an illicit relationship between Doc and Rio and between Billy and

Rio . . . the countless shots of Rio, in which her breasts are not fully covered." When a seal of approval was withdrawn from the film, industrialist-moviemaker Howard Hughes went ahead and showed it anyway, but state after state either banned the film or succeeded in getting certain scenes cut.

- *From Here to Eternity* (1951): In one of the best-known scenes in this popular movie about the peacetime army before World War II, Warden (Burt Lancaster) and Karen (Deborah Kerr) are shown embracing on the beach, both wearing bathing suits. The censors wanted the two to wear "a beach robe or some other type of clothing before they go into embrace." The moviemakers

The disrobing scene in "From Here to Eternity" raised the ire of the film's censors. *(Museum of Modern Art/Film Stills Archive)*

won out, the two lovers stayed in bathing suits, and the movie went on to win eight Academy Awards, including one as Best Movie of the Year.

- *A Streetcar Named Desire* (1951): Made from Tennessee Williams' Pulitzer Prize-winning play, *Streetcar* was one of the first pictures to treat the delicate subject of rape on the screen, the censor yielding to Williams' plea: "The rape of Blanche by Stanley is a pivotal, integral truth in the play, without which the play loses its meaning, which is the ravishment of the tender, the sensitive, the delicate, by the savage and brutal forces of modern society."

- *Spartacus* (1960): In one scene cut from the movie, a Roman general (Sir Laurence Olivier) is seen trying to acquire a male slave (Tony Curtis) for homosexual purposes.

Censorship doesn't only come from within. As we have seen in other chapters, the elusive thing called censorship takes many different forms and guises. Consider, for instance, the kind of censorship exerted when a pressure group organizes a boycott of a movie and forces the makers to either change the movie or withdraw it altogether. Is that not censorship? For regardless of how well-meaning the pressure group may be, it is exerting a force that without doubt *censors* the production from being what its makers had intended it to be. Here, concentrating again on the movie classics, are a few examples of this "invisible censorship":

- *The Caine Mutiny* (1954): In this film adaptation of the novel by Herman Wouk, the United States Navy refused to allow the filmmakers to photograph scenes aboard Navy ships, arguing that the Navy never had a mutiny and the film would project the "wrong idea" about the Navy. After a long battle, the Navy finally gave in, and producer-director Stanley Kramer summed up the situation: "I do not regard myself as a knight in shining armor. I won't say I don't have to fight. But basically, I am convinced the situation is loaded in my favor. For, while we tinker with freedom, we believe as a nation in freedom. And I don't believe in government censorship in any form."
- *Francis Goes to West Point* (1952): A talking mule? Not at the staid U.S. Military Academy, said the United States Army—the movie could not be made at the Point. Only when a General was taken on as a technical adviser to protect the interest of the Army was Francis the mule allowed at the Academy.
- *The Defiant Ones* (1958): Here the State Department argued with Kramer, contending that his submission of the film to the Berlin Film Festival was improper because it overemphasized bigotry in the United States. It was, in the words of the government, "not in the best interests of the United States." Kramer went ahead and showed the film anyway—to critical acclaim.

- *The Longest Day* (1962): In this film about the World War II D-Day invasion at Normandy, the government cut short the number of American troops it would allow in the film because of congressional protests against using American soldiers in a Hollywood movie. A case of indirect government censorship? Debatable perhaps, but by limiting the number of Americans, the government, however unintentional, was creating the impression that only a limited number of Americans played a part in the invasion.

If the major productions of the 1970s are not inspiring loud cries for censorship, many of the minor ones are. For pornographic films—known in the trade as "skin flicks"—are the products of an entire industry devoted especially to them. Most of the producers of these movies are fond of citing the "artistic" merits of their films, pointing to "the exploration of intense human relationships."

Regardless of the controversy surrounding the makers and showers of hard-core "sex movies," they claim the protection of the First Amendment too. As one owner of a theater which shows X-rated films put it: "I just stand by the principles of the First Amendment. An adult ought to be able to see whatever he wants to. No sex film ever hurt anybody."

When *Deep Throat* was banned as obscene from this theater owner's movie house, a citizen wrote to his local newspaper: "It's about time for some of these self-righteous do-gooders to realize that this is the latter part of the 20th century, and if adults want to spend their money viewing such films, it is their personal business. It does not infringe on the rights of others, no one forces anyone to view these films, and I'm sure minors are not allowed to enter such establishments. One might theorize that censorship merely serves to create curiosity as to what was censored."

Why, this person wanted to know, are "violent, bloody, and sadistic films" allowed to be shown on the screen, but "when it comes to mother nature, it's a no-no." He wrote: "We hear the voices of the pro-censorship groups constantly, so why don't we hear from those who object to being dictated to when it comes to what we may read or see? There must be two sides to this question."

On the other side, the so-called pornographic films have been blamed for everything from juvenile delinquency to a rise in venereal disease. A Maryland supporter of his state's censorship board said: "Birth control pills, venereal disease and illegitimacy are directly related to permissiveness and obscene movies."

Applying the Supreme Court guidelines for obscenity, a Washington, D.C. jury last year found the unedited version of *Deep Throat* obscene. After the jury viewed the movie and made its decision, D.C. Superior Court Judge Joseph M. Hannon took the unusual step of commenting on a jury verdict—by thanking the jurors "very much for defending decency here." (The manager of the theater which showed the film countered that he was shocked by the verdict: "The film was no worse, no better than any other [sex] film. I guess the jury never went downtown to see other sex films.")

When the Maryland Board of Censors banned *Deep Throat* as hard-core pornography, X-rated theater owners went on showing it anyway, despite a number of police raids. At first, a Baltimore City judge upheld the Board's ruling, then Maryland's Court of Appeals, the state's highest court, unanimously upheld the ban on the movie, asserting that: "In fact, *Deep Throat* would probably be deemed obscene under any meaningful definition of that term." Judge John C. Eldridge, who wrote the court opinion, said that more than half of the sixty-four-minute film was devoted to "a series of explicit depictions of sexual acts," and observed that, "It is noteworthy that in other jurisdictions where the matter has arisen, *Deep Throat* has consistently been found to be obscene."

Despite efforts by anticensorship forces to get legislation passed to abolish the board or to cut its budget, the censors have managed to survive. In October 1973 the Supreme Court by a 5-4 vote upheld the board's constitutionality (although controversies over decisions made by the board still continue).

Voicing the opinion of many who would like to see the state censors go, Senator Meyer M. Emanuel, Jr., said that parents should be able to control what movies their children view: "It's the parents who are seeing these (obscene) shows."

Over the years, communities in every state have fought hard to prevent theaters specializing in X-rated movies from opening. But most communities appear resigned to the idea that sex-oriented movies cannot be closed down forever. In many areas of the country, people blame the 1973 Supreme Court decision on obscenity for so confusing law enforcement authorities that they do not know what to do.

With the courts often not knowing what to do, people themselves appear to be becoming more and more apathetic toward pornography, and less and less outraged. A Chicago City Alderman, on finding an influx of adult theaters in his own Ward, complained: "The parking lot was full every night for two months with people coming in from outside. Most of our residents are family people and older folks and they just wouldn't go. Some sort of community protest is needed, but I don't see that at the moment. People don't know what to do."

In one of the most significant decisions to date affecting film censorship, the Supreme Court in June 1974 ruled (in *Jenkins v. Georgia*) that the X-rated movie *Carnal Knowledge* was not obscene. Unanimously reversing a lower court conviction of a Georgia theater owner who showed the film, the High Court in an opinion written by Justice William H. Renquist said that although *Carnal Knowledge* contained occasional scenes of nudity, "nudity alone is not enough to make material legally obscene under the Miller (*Miller v. California*) standards."

The landmark 1973 Miller case, you will recall, is the one in which the Supreme Court ruled that it is community concepts which determine whether or not a thing is obscene. The Jenkins opinion explained: "Miller held that it was constitutionally permissible to permit juries to rely on the understanding of the community from which they came as to contemporary community standards, and the states have considerable latitude in framing statutes under this element of the Miller decision."

While the High Court in 1974 ruled that *Carnal Knowledge* was not obscene, it left it up to the states and localities to decide what is or is not obscene. Justice William J. Brennan, Jr., commented after the Jenkins decision that it still "does not extricate us from the mire of case-by-case determinations of obscenity." A much stronger comment came from an executive of the American Booksellers Association who said the 1974 ruling "dumped a barge of sludge into already muddy waters."

Stage plays have also been challenged as obscene. In a 1975 ruling on the play *Hair*, the Supreme Court for the first time gave constitutional protection to live theater, holding that stage plays may not be censored in advance without strict safeguards that would protect First Amendment rights.

The Court did not describe the standards or measures that should be used in order to classify certain scenes as obscene, but it said that the same legal defenses that prevent books, movies, and other forms of expression from censorship also apply to live theater.

"Each medium of expression," said Justice Harry A. Blackmun's majority opinion, "must be assessed for First Amendment purposes by standards suited to it, for each may present its own problems." The musical *Hair*, he said, was entitled to protections "deeply etched in our law"—on the principle that "a free society prefers to punish the few who abuse rights of speech after they break the law than to throttle them and all others beforehand."

The case arose out of a ban on the musical by the city of Chattanooga, Tennessee, in 1972, and the subsequent upholding of the ban by lower federal courts which deemed the play obscene because of the nude scenes and simulated intercourse in it. It is important to note that the High Court, in its 5-4 ruling, did not judge whether the play was obscene but merely stressed that a play cannot automatically be banned because people may *think* it obscene; they first must take the case to court for a fair judicial hearing, and they must prove obscenity.

Justice William O. Douglas, who was among the dissenters and opposes any form of censorship, said the majority was merely applying "procedural Band-aids" to the problem; he was opposed to any legal action at all against *Hair*. Another who dissented, for a different reason, was Justice Byron R. White, who said the majority rule seemed to be compelling Chattanooga to let the show go on, with all its "simulated acts of anal intercourse, frontal intercourse, heterosexual intercourse, homosexual intercourse and group intercourse."

Did the High Court really resolve the problem of obscenity in theatrical presentations? By not defining what constitutes obscenity in a stage show, it probably did not, and it almost may be said with certainty, as one observer put it, that, "The issue will be back and will be back and will be back until something amounting to a Freedom of Private Pleasure Act becomes the law of the land."

Sex and violence are not the only themes that trouble would-be censors.

One of the biggest furors ever created by a film was set off by a short eighteen-minute color film called *The Lottery*, which its critics claimed destroyed the concept of mother love.

Based on a critically acclaimed short story of the same title by Shirley Jackson, first published in 1948 in *The New Yorker*, the controversial film, produced by the Encyclopaedia Britannica Educational Corporation, is an attempt to tell the story of man's inhumanity to man and of blind adherence to tradition for tradition's sake. To get this message across, the film depicts the citizens of an unnamed town in rural America who hold an annual lottery. The winner is a mother who is matter-of-factly stoned to death by the villagers—including the woman's own husband and children—as a sacrifice to some unnamed deity.

The idea of attacking tradition is at the heart of the meaning of the film, which was intended, as someone explained, to show how "a conventional community of well-intentioned citizens is likely to resist any challenge to whatever it may consider an inviolable tradition." Yet it is precisely this point that has aroused the most controversy, for the film's critics make an argument of the fact that it attacks traditional family values. They say it is "anti-Christian, anti-American, anti-parent, anti-everything"—as one complaining citizen told a reporter after the film was removed from schools by the Prince George's (Maryland) County Board of Education in 1974, a move that made the film a national *cause célèbre*.

The film's opponents said they were fighting for tradition, and against "humanists" and "bureaucrats" who they claimed were using the schools to alter or distort the belief of children.

Coming to the defense of the film have been ministers, teachers, parents, PTA presidents, and students who argue that it is only right that stagnant, unchanging tradition should be challenged. The American Civil Liberties Union (ACLU) contends that not only is this so, but that banning such a film violates the constitutional rights of teachers and students.

Criticizing the Prince George's County ban on the film, Pastor Thomas H. Conley of the University Baptist Church declared: "If the board is desperate to [ban] something, I bring to its attention a book that has violence and the slaughter of children, mothers eating their children in a time of siege; [it] has language that portrays rape, masturbation, the act of urination and incest. Its stories have a cultural milieu of child sacrifice. . . . If you must ban something, think of banning this book. It is the Old Testament."

It is a plain case of censorship to ban "The Lottery," claim others. John Gruber, president of the Prince George's County Educators Association, put it this way: "The indiscriminate censoring of curricular material is,

Stoning scenes in the controversial film of Shirley Jackson's story "The Lottery" were the subject of a heated debate over censorship. The movie's detractors

claimed it destroyed the concept of "mother love"; its defenders hailed it as illustrating the point of resistance to change.

(Encyclopaedia Britannica Educational Corporation)

the association believes, injurious to the quality of education in the county school system. We cannot and will not accept this. We will not condone censorship in any form . . . we will not and cannot condone the Joe McCarthy tactics."

On the other hand, several members of the board countered that those who oppose censorship are in fact the worst censors. One board member said: "Those who seem to make the loudest shouts of censorship would seek themselves to oppose, I feel, a most insidious act of censorship on the board itself, to censor the board for wanting to meet its responsibilities." Another board member added: "We keep hearing 'censorship,' which disturbs me, because what is censorship to some is nothing more than good judgment to others."

It is interesting to note that no one on the school board voted to ban the *written* story.

While almost all of the states have disallowed censorship boards, a number of communities across the country have stayed with them.

In Clarkstown, New York, for instance, a blind man sits as a censor of movies. Insensible, you say? How does he do it? The fact is that the man, Harry Snyder, sits with eight other seeing censors who fill him in when the screen goes silent, and he views pornography as not so much a case of seeing as a "case of feeling," which is a very interesting definition.

This may explain how the blind man does his job, but the story does not end there. Anticensorship forces, seeing the symbolism in it, have been prone to call Mr.

Snyder the "perfect censor," the "most sensible of all possible censors," and have gone so far even as to suggest that Clarkstown be given a Chamber of Commerce award as the "Wisest Town in the U.S.A."

A writer for *The New York Times,* commenting on the Clarkstown censor, and summing up the feelings of those who oppose the censorship of movies, put it succinctly when he said: "Censorship shelters the community from what it does not go to see. It is protection of the blind. It is right that it should be done by the blind."

6

Censorship and the Press

Will Lewis refused to give in. In 1974 two political radical groups, the Symbionese Liberation Army and the Weathermen, trusted him with evidence of great interest to law enforcement authorities: an original tape-recorded message containing the voice of the then wanted heiress Patricia Hearst, whom the authorities believed had joined the SLA, and a "Weather Underground" memo that discussed a bombing of the California state attorney general's office.

Relying on a California "newsman's shield" law designed to protect newsmen from making forced disclosures against their will, Lewis, manager of station KPFK in North Hollywood, California, refused to hand over the items to the authorities, who wanted them to see if they contained fingerprints. After Lewis refused to bow to two subpoenas ordering him to give up the evidence, he was held in contempt of court and given a jail sentence, a conviction upheld by the 9th U.S. Court

114

of Appeals which ruled that there was a legitimate law enforcement reason for the authorities' demand.

But Lewis still refused to give in, saying he would give up copies only, not the originals. He went to jail and spent two weeks there—thus joining the growing list of newspeople who say they would rather go to jail than buckle under to what they consider censorship of the free press in America.

The cornerstone of press freedom, the First Amendment, has been called (somewhat irreverently) a "Holy Writ of American journalism." But in the minds of many newsmen, the pressures being put to bear on them by the courts are changing the words of the amendment— from "Congress shall make no law respecting an establishment of religion, or prohibiting the free exercise

Safeguard against government censorship: the First Amendment to the Constitution. *(Gerald S. Snyder)*

thereof; or abridging the freedom of speech, or of the press . . ." to, in effect, Congress shall make *almost* no law respecting an establishment of religion, or prohibiting the free exercise thereof *except in certain circumstances;* or abridging the freedom of speech, or of the press *unless absolutely necessary* . . . (italics added). In other words, say the journalists, the First Amendment is being changed, if not in fact, then in spirit; and if federal officials have their way, it may even be altered to allow the courts to grant some access to the sources used by the news media. It is being argued that if the First Amendment means that anyone can print whatever he wishes, which was the intent of the Founding Fathers, it may be that today a form of censorship is being practiced on the news media—the press and television and radio newspeople.

Why is the news media under such heavy attack? Writing in the *Columbia Journalism Review,* newsman Ben H. Bagdikian answers the question this way:

The country has passed through more than a decade of radical change, in race relations, in assassinations of three national leaders [President John F. Kennedy, Senator Robert F. Kennedy and Martin Luther King], in a disastrous war, in lifestyles, in international strategy, all of it inevitably creating turbulence and confusion under the best of conditions. All of it was transmitted to the public by the news media. The news was real. The events would have occurred without the media. But they have made the media, the bearer of bad and disturbing news, a perfect scapegoat. The most powerful leaders of the country have done precisely this, turning public confusion and uneasiness about events against the press.

Newspeople, then, are bearers of bad tidings. Yet generally the press feels it has the right to print anything it deems is in the public interest. The First Amendment, after all, guarantees a free press, and this is essential to the democratic process.

But, as we have seen, serious problems are being raised by the press' attempts to carry out what it believes is its solemn responsibility—and the question of censorship lies at the heart of much of the problem. In this age of electronics and fast-moving news developments, for example, items of public interest come to the newspeople in multi-faceted forms, some of them through channels that may in fact even be considered illegal. A stolen document, for instance, might come to the attention of a newspaper but, in the newspaper's view, it might contain information that should be published.

Should it be published? If a court issues a temporary restraining order prohibiting a newspaper from publishing certain kinds of information, does this violate the free press protection guaranteed by the First Amendment? Where, if anywhere, does the people's right to know stop? Suppose a journalist is granted an exclusive interview with a fugitive from justice—on the condition that the journalist pledges not to turn the fugitive in to the police. The journalist feels that the interview will produce information valuable to the public. Should the journalist be free of any court action which would force him to reveal the whereabouts of the fugitive?

For a clue as to how the press feels about the crucial first question—should stolen material be published?—a group of journalists who gathered with judges, prosecutors, and lawyers at a Virginia workshop in 1975 agreed in large that a newspaper should *not* publish material stolen by one of its own reporters, but it might publish the material *if* someone else stole it and gave it to its reporter.

One of the attending journalists later remarked: "Some of the nonjournalists seemed to find this an interesting bit of tightrope walking."

As for the second question—do restraining orders violate the constitutional protection guaranteed to the press?—most judges feel such orders are needed to insure justice. Someone, they argue, must have the authority to say no, and that power lies with the judiciary—the courts—and not even the First Amendment can give absolute protection to journalists.

As you might imagine, there are no positive answers to these questions—only opinions by the press and by the courts. Due to differences of opinion, there have been many First Amendment court cases in recent years.

Because journalists are collectors of information and must rely on knowledgeable people to provide their information, they are dependent on their "sources," and guard them jealously. In order to get to the truth of a matter, they often rely on sources to reveal hidden facts, and the sources, in turn, often give the information on the proviso that their names not be disclosed. For in digging deeply for a story, the good newsman does not just accept what he has been told. If it is not merely "news" but "truth" that he is after, he knows he must pursue an *interpretation* of the events he is trying to describe. In what may be called "investigative journalism," the journalist uses his sources to go after the hard-to-get hidden truths behind an event—as did reporters Carl Bernstein and Bob Woodward of *The Washington Post* while presenting the truth about the Watergate scandal that forced President Nixon to resign from office.

There exists a real relationship between a reporter and his source. Journalists contend that if they are forced in court to testify about this relationship, the relationship itself will be harmed and continued information will be cut off, depriving the public of the information it should have. Journalists feel they must protect and, when necessary, conceal the identity of their sources.

Together with that other source of needed information —the "leak"—the good news source has become an essential ingredient of good journalism.

Sometimes a "good source" can land a journalist in trouble. In the words of one observer of the American press: "When journalists are presented with secret information about issues of great import, they become, in a very real sense, agents for the surreptitious source. Even if the disclosure is supported by authoritative documents, the journalist cannot know whether the information has been altered, edited, or selected out of context. Nor can he be certain what interest he is serving or what will be the eventual outcome of the leak."

Of course, journalists are not forced to use the material in the form it is given to them. By adding to or changing the material, they can put it into their own version. But because the courts feel that the art of keeping certain information from the law may in fact constitute a breaking of the law, journalists are getting into more and deeper trouble with the law.

In another California case, three staff members of the *Fresno Bee* were given jail terms for refusing to answer questions about the source of stories that gave in detail the testimony from a sealed grand jury transcript.

While newsmen continue to argue their right to protect confidential news sources, the ruling that still reigns supreme is a 1972 decision by the U.S. Supreme Court (the vote was 5-4) that said, the First Amendment notwithstanding, newsmen *cannot* refuse to reveal their sources if a grand jury orders that the sources be revealed. When it made the ruling (in the *Branzburg* decision), the Supreme Court indicated that it would closely follow future demands on newsmen. But as late as 1976 the Court has not commented further on its 1972 ruling—leaving the issue of newsmens' rights at the center of a broiling controversy.

The press views its responsibility as having to *inform* the public, fully and fairly, on all issues that are in the interest of the public. While the term "public interest" may be an abstraction and difficult to understand, there certainly are degrees of interest that the public has a right to know about. It is up to the press, journalists believe, more than any other organ of our society, to exert its constitutional right to make that interest known.

In the words of John B. Oakes, editor of the editorial page of *The New York Times,* "If we of the press do not in fact have the freedom guaranteed us by the First Amendment, we cannot in any meaningful way be responsible, either to our readership or to ourselves; and, conversely, if we of the American press do not hold ourselves responsible, we are not likely to hang on very much longer to our freedom."

It is time now to look closer at the First Amendment— a statement adopted, in the words of one of its best-known spokesmen, the former North Carolina Senator Sam J. Ervin, Jr., for two reasons: "to insure that Americans would be politically, intellectually and spiritually free," and to make certain "that our system of government, a system designed to be responsive to the will of an informed public, would function effectively."

If this is true, it follows that the Constitution gave the press the role to seek out the truth, which has meant over the decades the publishing of stories that are critical of the government, the Administration, and public institutions. The point is that the mere threat of a subpoena to testify before a governmental tribunal about the confidential source of a news story may be a very intimidating thing. Knowing that they might be subpoenaed or end up in jail could cause journalists to back off from going after a story that they otherwise might not hesitate to go after.

In effect then, as the journalists' argument has it, the press is being censored from carrying out the role the Constitution gave it. When this happens, says Sam Ervin, it is "the public which has lost information which could lead to political and social improvement . . . without the protection of anonymity, inside sources may simply dry up. The stories will not be written. We all will be the losers. And nobody—culprit or reporter—will go to jail."

What journalists are looking for to combat this are federal "shield" laws which would protect them from having to divulge the names of their sources. This is a most controversial issue, hotly debated by those who claim it could be used as a device behind which irresponsible reporters might hide. It is one thing to criticize, these people say, but the newsman must be held accountable for what he writes. Court orders must be obeyed. The press must not have unrestrained and unreviewable power.

On the other hand, those who favor shield laws point out that most proposals for their creation do not protect the newsman against claims of lawsuits for libel or slander. Therefore, the checks against irresponsible reporting would remain.

Whatever the pros and cons of shield laws, the ultimate idea seems a sound one—to unshackle the press from acts of intimidation which tend to suppress a free press.

As Senator Ervin once told the North Carolina Press Association:

A press which is not free to gather news without threat of ultimate incarceration cannot play its role meaningfully. The people as a whole must suffer. If the sources of that information are limited to official spokesmen within government bodies, the people have no means of evaluating the worth of their promises and assurances. The search for truth among competing ideas, which the First Amendment contemplates, would become a matter of reading official news releases. It is the responsibility of the press to insure that competing views are presented, and it is our responsibility as citizens to object to actions of the government which prevent the press from fulfilling this constitutional role.

It is not yet a federal crime for reporters to refuse to disclose the sources of their news stories (unless this is demanded by a grand jury). But there are people who would like to make it one. A proposal for legislation that would do this has been scored by some as, in effect, legislation that would act against the interests of the people. "If this had been the law three years ago," said Sen. Alan Cranston of California to the American Society of Newspaper Editors, "the public probably would never have gotten the full story of Watergate."

Taking another view, Chesterfield Smith, a past president of the American Bar Association, asserts that it is not upon shield laws but the First Amendment that newsmen must depend. Calling it the "most precious of our constitutional rights," Smith said the First Amendment, "protects reporters from disclosing the sources of their news stories to a greater extent than could any shield law. If a shield law gave greater protection, it seems to me right off that it would simply be unconstitutional. I therefore have opposed the adoption of any type of reporters' privilege act since I feel that the problem created by revelations of identities of 'confidential sources' of information should be dealt with by the courts on a case by case basis."

Few people will question that in recent years the use of court orders, subpoenas, search warrants, and police arrests all have served to force the disclosure of journalists' confidential sources and unpublished information. Asserted Arthur R. Taylor, president of CBS and chairman of the First Amendment Research and Defense Fund Campaign of the Reporters Committee for Freedom of the Press: "The alarming successful effort by some government officials . . . to misuse the power of the subpoena and the court order to silence the flow of information through the press to the public has resulted in a cumulative erosion of press freedom as never before witnessed under our Constitution."

In much stronger terms, one columnist recently charged that an "epidemic of news suppression" has hit the United States, causing a "vanguard of totalitarianism" to gain ground in America, while threatening the First Amendment, the freedom that proclaims the rights of Americans to speak their minds without the approval of the government.

How far does this right extend? If freedom of the press is guaranteed by the Bill of Rights, why does it always seem to be running into trouble?

The answer is that no right is *absolute;* it is up to the discretion of courts of law to interpret the extent to which the right applies, as the following brief roundup

The Bill of Rights—the first ten Amendments to the Constitution—guarantees every citizen protection against acts of censorship. *(Library of Congress)* of recent court skirmishes involving press censorship reveals:

- *Madisonville, Tennessee.* When Dan Hicks, Jr., editor of the weekly *Monroe County Observer*, published an article about a seventeen-year-old boy charged with murdering his uncle, County Judge J. P. Kennedy sentenced him to five days in the county jail and fined him $50 for violating an order that he not print anything about the case.

  Hicks, the winner of a number of national awards for courage in journalism, wrote in the *Observer* that Judge Kennedy's "so-called order not only operates to suppress me but it would put me under effective censorship."

- *Long Beach, California.* Is an ordinance banning newspapers with cover pictures of nudes from sidewalk vending machines constitutional or does it violate the First Amendment?

  "Constitutional," ruled Superior Court Judge R. J. Brown, who rejected an American Civil Liberties Union suit which had challenged the ordinance. "It seems strange," said the judge, "that people can be prohibited from smoking in certain areas because the smoke is unpleasant and offensive to others in the same place . . . and yet the government is powerless to prevent the kind of annoyance that comes from having to look at pictures that are repulsive, indecent."

- *Wyandotte, Michigan.* Can a judge attempt to

censor news accounts of a widely discussed rape case?

No, said Michigan District Court Judge Audrey Stroia, who reversed her own ruling against the *Wyandotte Guardian News-Herald,* ordering a reporter and photographer removed from a hearing on the case. The judge issued the reversal after the paper's general manager argued that the case was well known in the area and the judge had allowed spectators to remain in the court.

- *Washington, Ohio.* Does a reporter have the right to publish the name of a trial witness named in open court?

  No, ruled Fayette County Common Pleas Court Judge Evelyn W. Coffman in a case involving *Washington Court House Record-Herald* reporter Thomas E. Summers. But overruling its decision was Union County Common Pleas Court Judge Gwynn Sanders, who said Judge Coffman had exceeded her authority. Declared Judge Sanders: "This court is of the opinion that a judge has no right to gag the press for reporting actions which occur in the courtroom."

- *High Point, North Carolina.* If newspapers are permitted to cover city council hearings into charges of alleged corruption by the police department, shouldn't radio and television reporters also have that right?

  Indeed they should, ruled the North Carolina Court of Appeals in overruling a lower court judge who barred radio and television recording of the hearing. In the unanimous Court of Appeals decision, Judge Edward B. Clark said, "The different treatment of competing forms of communication is hardly justified."

In most cases, most public newspapers exert a great deal of self-censorship—if the term "censorship" is used in the sense of self-control. Knowing, for instance, that the printing of "dirty words" will surely provoke reader protests, most newspapers try to avoid them, using them only if the editors feel they are absolutely essential to the story. If the questionable words are necessary in order to create a needed fact or to help build a certain mood to put the story into proper perspective, they might be used. But editors often will clash among themselves over the degree of need to use dirty words.

When one editor, Charles Alexander of the *Dayton (Ohio) Journal Herald,* allowed a vulgar word to be printed in the story of a Treasury agent who killed a colleague in a heated debate over which one was to receive a transfer, the newspaper's management rebuked him, and he resigned. In a column he wrote before he left, Alexander explained:

To me the telling of that message [that people must use restraint or they will destroy themselves] from an incident of real life, including in one instance the raw vulgarity used by a man blind with rage, is a lesson that every man, woman and child should perceive in all its dimensions. . . . The complaints we received had nothing to do with introducing a word into the culture, much less into the language.

The objection was to putting it into print. I did not approve its publication lightly. I would have preferred to avoid it. As a matter of practice, it is not done at all on this newspaper unless it is deemed unavoidable. But if it seems unavoidable, I question that the basic cause of decency is served by playing euphemistic games. "You don't have to print the word because every one knows that goes in there anyway," I was told by several callers.

If its use in print contaminates children—and I am amazed at the number of children under 12 who, according to parents, read the paper from cover to cover—I would hope that parents would have the depth to realize that the real lesson here is not so much that the word in question is never used—children know better—but that intemperate language is often a prelude to intemperate behavior and tragedy. Language is the verbal expression of man's condition, not the source of it. Language is amoral . . . I am not a champion of dirty words. I am a champion of the press trying, as the opportunity presents itself, to give mankind a telling insight into its own frailty. . . .

Today the press is seeking to strengthen its credentials. While coming under very severe attacks, in both the minds of the public and in the courts, the press continues to exert its power—the power to inform and to insure that one of the most important guarantees of the Constitution remains intact: the guarantee of freedom of expression.

7

Students' Rights

In December 1965 a group of students and adults in Des Moines, Iowa, gathered for a meeting at the home of sixteen-year-old high school student Christopher Eckhardt, and decided that to voice their objections to the Vietnam War, the students would wear black armbands to school, as symbols of their feelings.

When school officials heard of the plan, they also met, and, fearing a disturbance, vowed to temporarily oust from school any student who wore the armbands and refused to remove them. They charged that such action constituted disruptive conduct.

The students were aware of the newly-adopted regulations, but they wore the armbands anyway. They were sent home, and five were suspended; but through their fathers they filed a complaint in the United States District Court that claimed the students' constitutional rights to free expression had been violated. The court disagreed, and upheld the action of the school administrators on the ground that the restrictive order was a reasonable measure taken to prevent a breakdown in school discipline.

130

But still the students persisted. They appealed the case. They lost again, in the Court of Appeals for the Eighth Circuit. They appealed again, this time to the highest court in the land. And this time, in 1969, after a fight that had lasted for almost four years, they won, prompting a decision with far-reaching implications for the issue of censorship in the nation's schools.

Making sure that the First Amendment protected students in high school, the U.S. Supreme Court ruled (in *Tinker v. Des Moines Independent Community School District*) that, in the words of Justice Abe Fortas, who delivered the opinion of the Court:

First Amendment rights, applied in light of the special characteristics of the school environment, are available to teachers and students. It can hardly be argued that either students or teachers shed their constitutional rights to freedom of speech or expression at the schoolhouse gate. This has been the unmistakable holding of this Court for almost 50 years. . . . The school officials banned and sought to punish petitioners for a silent, passive, expression of opinion, unaccompanied by any disorder or disturbance on the part of petitioners. There is here no evidence whatever of petitioners' interference, actual or nascent, with the school's work or of collision with the rights of other students to be secure and to be let alone. Accordingly, this case does not concern speech or action that intrudes upon the work of the school or the rights of other students.

The decision was a momentous one, the most clear-cut statement on the constitutional rights of students in all schools throughout the United States. However, it is only when one reads further in the decision called *Tinker* that it becomes absolutely clear that the decision related not only to the wearing of armbands, but rather to all forms of expression in schools:

> In our system, state-operated schools may not be enclaves of totalitarianism. School officials do not possess absolute authority over their students. Students in school as well as out of school are "persons" under our Constitution. They are possessed of fundamental rights which the State must respect, just as they themselves must respect their obligations to the State.
>
> In our system, students may not be regarded as closed-circuit recipients of only that which the State chooses to communicate. They may not be confined to the expression of those sentiments that are officially approved. In the absence of a specific showing of constitutionally valid reasons to regulate their speech, students are entitled to freedom of expression of their views.

So, said the Court, the Constitution says that Congress (and the states) may not abridge the right to free speech, and "this provision means what it says." But it is important, too, to note that the Constitution does not say that this right is absolute; as the Supreme Court has interpreted it, the guarantee against the abridgement of the right to free speech does "permit reasonable regulation of speech-connected activities in carefully restricted circumstances."

While students have the right to express their opinions on any subject, they may lose that right if their action is clearly "disruptive." They may have to go to court to prove that the action was not disruptive. In some cases, students have been prevented from wearing armbands or buttons or from distributing student newspapers or literary magazines.

While the interpretation of the *Tinker* ruling may vary from state to state, the *Tinker* formula generally has held up.

In spite of the ruling, may material—be it a button, a mimeographed sheet, an underground newspaper, or a notice put on a bulletin board—ever be "censored" by school officials? Yes, but only *if* that material "materially and substantially" disrupts school activities, and if the authorities can prove this is the case. In other words, there still must be discipline and order in the schools— a theme repeatedly emphasized by the High Court, in affirming the need for a certain degree of control and conduct in the schools.

If the cry of "censorship" is heard with greater frequency today in the schools, it is because the trend is toward liberalized legal standards; the expansion, mainly, of rights of expression in student newspapers. In line with the new liberalization, and the outspokenness of the nation's press in general, student papers are reflecting a high degree of openness about controversial or previously taboo subjects.

At the same time, boards of education are continuing

to hold out the right to make "ultimate decisions" about the subject matter of student newspapers, paying closer attention than ever to stories which, because of their outspokenness, may be libelous, obscene, or disruptive. The administrators argue that the schools are, after all, responsible to the community, and therefore they should reflect the same sense of morality and good taste expected of the community in general.

Is this policy unconstitutional in that it denies students the rights of free speech enjoyed by their peers? Some teachers think it is, as do many students, but others think it is not, and opt for limited censorship of articles that fall into the libelous-obscene-disruptive category.

In 1973, the 7th U.S. Court of Appeals upheld the contention of the publishers of a student "underground" newspaper, the *Corn Cob Curtain*, which in 1972 was distributed in a number of Indianapolis high schools. When school authorities, angered by the use of certain four-letter words and "filthy cartoons," refused to continue to allow the newspaper to be distributed, the six student publishers went to court, claiming that their constitutional rights had been violated.

The students won the case, but the authorities took it to the United States Supreme Court, citing the school board rules against the distribution of anonymous literature.

In the arguments before the High Court, the issue of censorship was laid bare.

Arguing that "filth" must be weeded out of high school newspapers, the lawyer for the schools, Mrs. Lila J. Young, pleaded that school administrators be allowed "to take a peek and see what's coming into our schools. If you decide the schools can do nothing about this, then students will use this language and say 'The Supreme Court said we could.' If we have to set aside a time and a place in our schools for the distribution of this filth, then we are contributing to the delinquency of minors. If you decide school officials can do nothing about this, then many basic functions of our schools will be destroyed—among them, teaching how to use language properly and in socially acceptable terms."

Taking the other view, the students' lawyer, Craig E. Pinkus, responded, "These words are in the newspapers —*The New York Times,* the *Wall Street Journal,* in stories about presidential tapes; they are in novels like *The Catcher in the Rye.*"

The High Court refused to rule in the case, declaring that the graduation of the student editors rendered the case moot. Only Justice Douglas argued that the Court should have ruled anyway.

It is primarily the question of what is or is not "disruptive" that forces so many cases to court:

- *Columbus, Ohio.* When the Reynoldsburg High School student newspaper criticized athletic coaches for allowing players to drink and smoke, and also scored Columbus police for their handling of a rock concert, the principal halted the distribution of the edition containing the offending items. The edition should be burned, he said. The school board backed him, and later the principal ordered that the newspaper would have to submit all copy to him for prior approval before it could print again.

On behalf of the students, the American Civil Liberties Union brought suit—and lost. U.S. District Court Judge Carl Rubin declared that the controversial edition was disruptive. The U.S. Court of Appeals, however, deemed this decision "clearly in error," and ordered the case back to Rubin. Judge Rubin thought again, and reversed his earlier stand, this time voting in favor of the students, and asserting that if material published in high school student newspapers does not substantially interfere with school discipline, the papers cannot be censored.

Judge Rubin, in backing the students, ordered administrators at the high school to produce guidelines that spelled out what students may publish or "may not" publish.

- *Brooklyn, New York.* An edition of the *Paper Lion*, the Farmingdale High School newspaper, was confiscated by the school's administrators after a supplement contained in the paper discussed such subjects as contraception, abortion, and other sexual matters.

The students obtained an attorney, went to court, and won—U.S. District Court Judge Mark Constantino ruling that the students were right in their contention that the seizure was "an interference with student speech" and a violation of their constitutional rights. Rejecting the school officials' argument that information in the supplement was covered by a subject in the school curriculum, and therefore constituted an interference with their authority, Judge Constantino declared: "It is extremely unlikely that distribution of the supplement will cause material and substantial interference with school work and discipline. In this court's opinion, no clear and present danger is presented."

• *Baltimore, Maryland.* Claiming their First Amendment rights violated, the student Woodlawn Senior High School publishers of two private newspapers, the *Woodlawn Lampoon* and *Today's World,* gained the backing of the ACLU in a federal court suit against school authorities who had ordered distribution of the newspapers halted.

After a series of court tests, the U.S. Court of Appeals for the Fourth Circuit supported the students, removing any form of prior censorship on student newspapers. "We have both compassion and understanding of the difficulties facing school administrators," the court said, "but we cannot permit those conditions to suppress the First Amendment rights of individual students. Nor will any intolerable burden result from our decision. Indeed it may ameliorate the relationship between the student and the disciplinarian and lead them to empathize with each other."

Of course, students don't always win when they take their case to court. Witness the following as illustrations:

- *Long Beach, California.* Two allegedly obscene words from an anonymous "Mr. Long Hair" to the student editor of the *Rising Star* in the Long Beach Unified School District prompted school officials to ban the offending issue. When the editor and seven other students sought legal action, the officials charged that the *Rising Star* was attempting to "use the First Amendment as a cloak to show contempt and disrespect for school officials."

  The paper's legal counsel conceded in court that the two words were indeed "vulgar and profane," but said that they did not contain the sexual connotation that higher courts usually apply to find such words obscene.

  Superior Court Judge Roy J. Brown disagreed, denying an injunction against the school district and declaring that it was the officials' right to ban the publication from the school grounds. Upholding state guidelines and rules governing student expression, his ruling meant that student newspapers would still have to be submitted to the district for approval for publication—a procedure the students had charged violated the spirit of the U.S. Supreme Court when it upheld the publication of the Pentagon Papers by *The New York Times.*

  Replied the judge: "Public school cases involving freedom of the press have been viewed differently by the courts."

- *Ogden, Utah.* A photo showing the backs of two nude boys streaking, accompanying an article on the subject, prompted administrators at Bonneville High School to confiscate issues of the student newspaper, *The Beacon.*

There was no court action in the case, but a student, in a letter to the editor of the *Ogden Standard-Examiner,* expressed her indignation at the attempt at censorship: "We are in school to learn. Friday, we learned to disallow people to have differences of opinion with us. We learned that others do not have the right to have different tastes from ours. We learned that we must stifle our creativeness unless it appeals to the administration. We leaned that the Soviet Union was right in its censorship of Alexander Solzhenitsyn."

- *Potomac, Maryland.* Do high school officials have the right to censor student newspapers for libel or obscenity?

Yes, they do have that constitutional right, ruled the U.S. Court of Appeals in Richmond. But the court made it clear that prior restraint may not be imposed on students under the guise of any set of censorship regulations. There may be regulations governing student publications, but the regulations must be explicit enough so that a student can tell what he may or may not write.

The ruling, which grew out of a dispute be-

tween the parents of six Winston Churchill High
School students and school officials of Montgomery County, who objected to a position paper
written by the students that criticized the school's
censorship code, also made clear that high school
officials must promptly approve or disapprove of
student-edited material and, if disapproved, there
must be proper and prompt appeals procedures.

The court asserted: "While school authorities
may ban obscenity and unprivileged libelous material, there is an intolerable danger, in the context of prior restraint, that under the guise of such
vague labels, they may unconstitutionally choke
off criticism, either of themselves, or of school
policies. . . . That they may not do."

• *Ipswich, Massachusetts.* Members of the English
department of Ipswich High School came to the
aid of student editors of the *Tiger's Tale* after
the bimonthly publication stirred up a controversy
with an issue devoted to sex and sexual attitudes.

When parents, anti-abortionists, and others in
the small North Shore town denounced the issue
as biased and "inappropriate" for public high
school students, the English teachers acted to
head off threatened censorship of future issues
by a school committee, vowing to take to court
any efforts at prior restraint on what the students
could say.

In the issue, the *Tiger's Tale* had reported the
results of a poll and interviews of one hundred

students, which showed that fifty-two had participated in intercourse, and of these only sixteen had used contraceptives. The co-authors of the edition, upon finding the low use of contraceptives, had interviewed two local specialists in the field of sex and pregnancy, and presented in the issue information about modern contraceptive devices and sex education courses offered by the school.

• *Fresno, California.* When an article on marijuana that included the results of a student survey on the use of the controversial narcotic, in addition to an interview with a physician who commented on the effects of marijuana, appeared in an issue of *The Hatchet,* a student news magazine of Washington Union High School, it was suppressed by the superintendent, and his decision was backed by the board of trustees.

The story's authors had said, "It is not the position of *The Hatchet* to condone or condemn the use of marijuana, but only to provide the statistics on this problem." But because the magazine did not editorialize against the use of marijuana, said the *Hatchet*'s editor, the superintendent was upset. He ordered all copies locked up in the newspaper office, and said the administration would pay for reprinting the entire issue without the offending article.

The magazine's faculty advisor disagreed with this action, calling the article "objective and responsible," but at least one of the trustees complained that it has "no redeeming social value." It was the same thing as pornography, the trustee said.

• *Gresham, Oregon.* When teacher Marilyn Schultz refused to endorse the newspaper code of ethics at Centennial High School, calling it unconstitutional and unworkable, she was relieved of her journalism responsibilities.

Two district journalism advisors had prepared the code, and it had been accepted by the school's administration. But Mrs. Schultz said that because the code states that "the newspaper will refrain from printing any unkind references about individuals," it prevents students from making constructive criticism in editorials and even in letters to the editor.

Generally the courts have supported this idea—and not just in high schools, but for all levels of the student press. In a leading college case (*Dickey v. Alabama State Board of Education*), Gary Dickey, the student editor at Troy State College, printed the word "censored" across a blank editorial column after his newspaper adviser objected to an editorial which urged politicians in the state to stop attacking the president of the University of Alabama for refusing to censor a student publication. The Troy State College president was shown Dickey's editorial and claimed that the student newspaper could not criticize state officials since they were the owners-publishers of the publication.

In place of the controversial editorial, Dickey was urged by his advisor to run a harmless substitute: "Raising Dogs in North Carolina." When he chose instead to run the word "censored," he was suspended from school.

Taking his case to the Federal District Court, Dickey won. Judge Frank M. Johnson, Jr., declared that unreasonable rules and regulations could not force him to give up "his constitutionally protected right of freedom of expression." He could not be prevented from exercising "his constitutionally granted right of academic and/or political expression."

Giving the final word on the subject of censorship and students' rights to the Supreme Court, it is interesting to note that apprehension or *fear* of disruption is no excuse for the exercise of censorship—no reason to overcome the right to freedom of expression. In the views of some, "any departure from absolute regimentation may cause trouble. Any variation from the majority's opinion may inspire fear. Any word spoken, in class, in the lunchroom or on the campus, that deviates from the views of another person, may start an argument or cause a disturbance."

The Constitution says we must take this risk, stated the Court. "Our history says that it is this sort of hazardous freedom—this kind of openness—that is the basis of our National strength and the independence and vigor of Americans who grow up and live in this relatively permissive, often disputatious society."

8

Censorship and the "Facts of Life"

In a memorandum in February 1975, the superintendent of a large metropolitan school system in the Midwest suddenly surprised his teachers by declaring that "effective immediately, no teaching, advising, directing, suggesting or counseling of birth control or abortion" would be permitted in the public schools. Backing traditional family roles, the superintendent urged that, instead, the teaching of such values as the preservation of the family unit be taught. He praised the feminine role of "wife, mother, and homemaker," the masculine role of "guide, protector, and provider," and called it the job of parents, not public schools, to educate children about birth control and abortion.

Many others agree. In a small Illinois community, a minister fighting against the public school use of materials dealing with human sexuality declared, "We will not give up, because the Bible says the authority to teach about sex is given to parents, not the schools." He pointed to Sweden where, he claimed, sex education has resulted in unwanted pregnancies, venereal disease, alcoholism, and "insanity" (a "totally uncalled for and unsupported claim," said a sex education expert in reply).

In the 1968-69 school year, at a time when the movement against sex education was at its peak, a group called Concerned Parents of Family Life Education Program Committee in Illinois sent a letter to parents containing the following warning:

We are again warning the Board of Education that if this Sex Education Program is adopted by the Board, we shall block any proposed increase in taxes earmarked for this school system. We now have sufficient members and finances to contact every family in School District 96, and expose this fraud perpetrated on the young minds of our children. We will spare no efforts to protect our children from this sinister plot to subvert their minds. You will have no tax increase when parents know how you are wasting their money, and at the same time twisting the minds of innocent children.

As a result of attacks made on school sex education programs, more than a dozen states have canceled or curtailed these programs. Almost two dozen states have been urged to adopt legislation that would prohibit sex education in the public schools; and in at least six states there have been court cases brought by organized groups seeking to restrict sex education in the public schools.

Here is a sampling of recent controversies over school sex education courses:

- *Fairfax County, Virginia.* When school authorities announced a sex education program for 5th through 12th graders—as a chance to "take sex out of the closet"—so many parents objected to the curriculum materials that the school board unanimously voted to put sex back in the closet, and to withdraw the proposal. "I am convinced that we must go back to the drawing board," said the county's school superintendent.

  Particular objection was leveled at films on venereal disease for intermediate level students, which the board found "unacceptable to the community."

- *Montgomery County, Maryland.* A slide-tape presentation on birth control entitled "Family Planning: Decisions and Methods" prompted some parents to complain to the school board; but by a 4-3 vote the board defeated a motion to ban the presentation, used in an optional four-to-eight day course on contraception for senior high school students.

- *Wentzville, Missouri.* Because a sex education speaker distributed copies of *Zing Comics—Ten Heavy Facts of Life* to junior high school students, the Wentzville teacher who had invited the speaker to address the students was suspended by the Wentzville Board of Education. Parents complained that the literature distributed by the speaker, who was from the Urban League of St. Louis, was pornographic.

The suspension was later reversed by the district's attorney who ruled that it was illegal to suspend the teacher without first giving her the right of a hearing to discuss the problem.

• *Churchville, New York.* Unhappy about sex education books in the junior high school library, particularly the books *Boys and Sex* and *Girls and Sex,* a member of the Churchville-Chili School Board resigned, charging these books and others with "endorsing sexuality."

The school board, however, refused to take any action on the case, refusing, in the words of one member, "to get into book censorship." She said, "Our staff is well qualified and we follow their opinions."

• *New York, New York.* When a Bronx high school teacher showed an all-girl biology class a film-strip called "Lovemaking," which included frames of a couple engaged in intercourse, the school chancellor reprimanded him and transferred him to a different school. Before the transfer, the move had been upheld by a U.S. District Court judge. But a New York district attorney dropped the investigation of the teacher, after complaining that "you can legally show in a school pictures that you can be locked up for showing to youths in a public theater."

> Part of a ten-unit sex education program written by a New York University professor, the filmstrip was produced by the Unitarian Universalist Association of Boston. "This was not an obscene, X-rated movie," the teacher said. "What I showed was an educational filmstrip . . . shown all through the U.S. to junior high school teenagers in their Sunday school sex education program."

Among the more extremist attacks on sex education, Robert Welch, director and founder of the John Birch Society wrote in 1969 that sex education was a "filthy Communist plot." A California extremist is reported to have urged a group he was addressing, "Go to school board meetings in your towns and other towns. Applaud and groan at the right times, and if necessary stomp your feet and scream . . . the more brazen you are, the more attention you'll get . . . it infuriates people in the program when you refer to it as a 'sex program.' It'll upset them, and when they're upset, they don't think so well."

Viewing such attempts at censorship, the National Education Association's Commission On Professional Rights and Responsibilities declared that "the irresponsible claims of extremists are succeeding in destroying carefully developed and constructive sex education programs in a number of American communities." While recognizing the concern of parents to protect their children from possibly unhealthy influences, the Commission contends that the campaign to abolish sex education "seeks to exploit" these natural anxieties and concerns. The Commission has declared: "At the heart of the right-wing attacks are unfounded allegations, innuendos, trumped-up charges, sensationalism, and blatant lies. Without ever really examining the specific merits or possible deficiencies of an existing local school system's program—an approach which could be truly constructive—extremists seek to destroy it entirely. If such groups are successful, the effect will be to deny the advantages of constructive programs of family life and sex education to present and future generations of children."

Attacks against sex education do not fall into the normal category of "censorship." But it is clear, as noted by Dr. Mary S. Calderone, M.D., President of the Sex Information and Education Council of the United States (SIECUS), that in this area "vocal, well-heeled and ultra-conservative minority groups can exert a kind of censorship."

Advancing the idea that many extremist groups that oppose sex education are not really interested in the issue at all, a director of Christian education for the Southern Presbyterian Church suggested that what these groups want most of all is power. "In dealing with these people," he told a meeting of the Charleston (W. Va.) Ministerial Association, "we are not dealing with persons who believe in dialogue. They are only interested in power. . . . Radical groups opposing sex education are not interested in the issue, but have found a vehicle with which to gain popularity and financial support."

The argument against sex education has become a

tirade. Yet before we go much further, it must be made clear that not all people who oppose the teaching of sex education in the public schools are extremists or use extremist tactics. It is quite the opposite. Many of the antisex education forces are genuine in their belief that the so-called "family life programs" which teach sex education have no place at all in the public schools. They are sincere in their fear that pornography is introduced into the classroom via sex education; that sex education should not be taught without the teaching of religious morality; and that sex education should be left to the family. Another fear that often leads to attempts to restrict or censor sex education programs stems from the belief that the sexual impulse is so strong that any recognition given to it in a discussion will only produce sexual stimulation and desires. Still another, more extremist contention is the one that holds sex education to be a "Communist plot." The fact is, however, that regardless of the arguments or the degrees of genuine concern, the issues often become confused. They frequently become part of a general attack on sex education, one that its proponents—who include clergymen, legislators, civic leaders, parents, and students themselves—see as disruptive to an equally genuine attempt to instill proper sexual guidance in young persons.

Why the current furor over sex education? In the first place, we must realize that attitudes toward sex have changed, and all the time they are continuing to change. Decades ago, parents prepared their children to be the same kind of adults as they were. But today we are a mixed society, composed of peoples of many different backgrounds and beliefs, and strengthened by the advances of science and a better understanding of human behavior.

Young people cannot be expected to behave or react like their grandparents. As an anthropologist explained:

We used to deal with sex as wicked; in fact everything connected with the body was wicked! And everything that *looked* as if it were connected with the body was pretty wicked. So, you never looked inside mother's handbag; and the insides of clothes closets were forbidden, and the inside of the icebox was horrible. Today people have bought plastic handbags, brightly lit refrigerators, and have clothes closets specially lit so that people who come to dinner can look in and see their hostesses' clothes. We've gone in for a tremendous illumination of all things that were once forbidden and dark.

People also are no longer as offended as they used to be by pictures of nudes in magazines, or even by premarital sex. According to a Gallup Poll on the subject, "In terms of attitudes on premarital sex, two out of every three Americans four years ago held the view that premarital sex relations are 'wrong.' Today, the public is closely divided, with 48 percent believing sex before marriage is wrong and 43 percent holding the opposite opinion."

This does not mean, however, that a large majority of

persons over the age of thirty do not, in fact, still view premarital sex as wrong; a majority of the thirty-plus group still say they are offended by the show of nudity in magazines and public places. As the Gallop Poll put it: "The puritan ethic continues to have a strong hold on the thinking of most Americans."

Adults generally do want sex education for their children, however. According to another Gallop Poll, 71 percent of all adults questioned favored sex education in the schools, and 55 percent of those questioned favored discussions of birth control in these courses. In addition, the survey indicated that Roman Catholics were almost as likely as Protestants to approve of sex education courses discussing birth control. A strong factor apparently influencing this support is the belief that too often the family environment does not provide adequate sex education to young people and, without this, they tend to "get the word" from the wrong places.

In a Purdue University poll, for instance, it was disclosed that of 1,000 teenagers questioned, 53 percent of the boys and 42 percent of the girls learned about the facts of human sexuality from their friends. While 35 percent of the girls said they received sex education from their parents, only 15 percent of the boys said this was the case. In general, 15 percent of the boys and girls said they "pieced things together" from sources that included television, movies, books, and pornographic materials. Some 6 percent noted that they received instruction from school, and 7 percent said they were advised by adults other than parents.

Sex education as such is not new. In one form or another, it has been taught in American elementary and secondary schools for decades, starting as strictly biological information about reproduction, and over the years maturing until today it goes by a multitude of names: Life Science and Human Development or Family Life and Human Development, to cite just two. Separate classes for boys and girls are usually held, but with identical material presented in the separate classes. If any parent wishes that his or her youngster not participate in the program or a particular portion of the course, the parent sends a letter to the principal. In some communities, plans have been worked out where, as a teacher explained, "a parent who objects has some way his child can opt out without being embarrassed."

It is impossible to guess how many sex education programs are offered in public and parochial schools in the United States today. Because of the autonomy of the schools, the programs are known to differ from school to school. As yet, nobody has surveyed them all to determine exactly how much or what quality of sex education is being taught, and where. Even a probability sample has not been taken. In one school, the curriculum might follow one pattern, and in another it might follow a different pattern altogether. It might be, as one physician-educator explained, "that they showed the film on menstruation to the girls in the gym on a rainy day, or it might mean a fully-developed, fine program that took five years to develop."

Usually, however, the basic facts of reproduction are

taught from kindergarten through the first five grades, with dating behavior and the emotional and physical changes of puberty taught to students in grades six through nine; and the psychological and moral aspects of sex taught in the higher grades.

To most people, the term "sex education" means teaching about the act of sex, or giving facts about reproduction, when, in fact, it means far, far more. For the very broad field of sexuality has to do with the whole person —what it means to be a man or a woman, a husband or wife, or a parent in all aspects of behavior.

"The critics," says Dr. Calderone, one of America's most respected physicians, who helped found SIECUS in 1964, "say that we are trying to teach pornography and homosexuality and masturbation in the classroom!"

Quite the contrary, she asserts. Sex education teaches that the sex act is an aspect of personality related to emotional and social adjustment, and that success or failure in fitting life into the "right" sex role, and properly conducting it, can lead to individual happiness, happiness as a family member, and real human fulfillment. When sex education concentrates only on "reproduction education," or biological information, it is not complete, because it does not consider the whole, growing person; it considers only the biological and not the *psychological* factors affecting personality.

A 1974 position statement by the directors of SIECUS declared that "Free access to full and accurate information on all aspects of sexuality is a basic right for everyone, children as well as adults."

In order that there be no misunderstanding about

what SIECUS sees as the desirable objectives of sex education, it will be worthwhile to look at the following SIECUS nine-point discussion:

1. To provide for the individual an adequate knowledge of his own physical, mental, and emotional maturation processes as related to sex.
2. To eliminate fears and anxieties relative to individual sexual development and adjustments.
3. To develop objective and understanding attitudes toward sex in all of its various manifestations—in the individual and in others.
4. To give the individual insight concerning his relationships to members of both sexes and to help him understand his obligations and responsibilities to others.
5. To provide an appreciation of the positive satisfaction that wholesome human relations can bring in both individual and family living.
6. To build an understanding of the need for the moral values that are essential to provide rational bases for making decisions.
7. To provide enough knowledge about the misuses and aberrations of sex to enable the individual to protect himself against exploitation and against injury to his physical and mental health.
8. To provide an incentive to work for a society in which such evils as prostitution and illegitimacy, archaic sex laws, irrational fears of sex, and sexual exploitation are nonexistent.
9. To provide the understanding and conditioning

that will enable each individual to utilize his sexuality effectively and creatively in his several roles, e.g., as spouse, parent, community member, and citizen.

The antisex education forces reply that perhaps these should be the objectives of sex education, but that this teaching belongs not in the school but in the home. The prosex education forces state simply that, if done at all, this is being done inadequately. The argument rages not so much over the *need* for sex education (although there are many people who would probably even debate that), but over who should do the sex educating, and in what style or manner. The criticism, however, does not stop here; it includes attacks by many individuals and groups who claim that sex education materials are really "smut" materials, or are "immoral" and "destructive of religious belief," or are "undermining the morals of American youth."

Answering the main charges, SIECUS maintains it is impractical to confine sex education to the home, "because parents are inadequately prepared to undertake this responsibility." It is simply too complex a subject. "No one or two persons can be adequately prepared in a cosmos that has become as complex and as varied as is today's world. This is what makes sex education confined to the home less effective than that derived from many sources."

The concensus among teachers is that even well-educated parents often never get around to having a meaningful discussion about the "facts of life" with their children, because a) they simply do not know how; b) they feel uncomfortable discussing the subject with their children; or c) they keep putting it off for so long that by the time they get around to it, they find that their children have learned, in their own way, what the parents were going to tell them in their way.

Are sex education courses "destructive of religious belief?"

Not if the reported effects of an "About Your Sexuality" course offered by the Unitarian-Universalist churches are to be believed. Reporting on this course, an instructor said findings have disclosed that the eleven to nineteen-year olds who take it become more liberal in their sexual attitudes. But, she explained, "they believe sexually related behavior to be a matter of individual choice rather than something which should be regulated by society through public law. The basic sexual standards by which an adolescent guides his sexual behavior remain unchanged as a result of sex education."

She found that the course did not lead to promiscuous sexual behavior, and the presentation of specific information regarding birth control and venereal disease did not lead to the removal of all inhibitions. "Sex-educated adolescents still cite fear of pregnancy or disease as major deterrents to sexual relations."

The results of church-related sex education courses, if the above example is taken as typical, are very positive, and contradict the charge that such courses often lead to promiscuous sexual behavior. "An overwhelming majority of adolescents believed sex should be associated with love relationships," reported one official.

In the public schools, some of these institutions view sex education as so important that they are revising and expanding their sex education curriculums, extending them to offer voluntary after-school self-defense classes for female students—with a view to instructing students to help avoid sexual attacks.

Overlooked in all of the discussion and controversy surrounding sex education is the need for sex education for parents. Don't parents also have the right to knowledge about human sexuality? To assume just because they are parents that they already know all there is to know is wrong, and so perhaps they too should be allowed the free, uncensored right to be informed, the prosex education people argue. Many of the harshest critics of sex education, it is claimed, never received proper childhod sex education themselves.

Summing up the effects of improper or inadequate sex education, the *Washington Star* asserted: "The drive [to destroy sex education] must not succeed. For the alternative to proper, controlled and accurate sex education is the back alley and the washroom, with its guaranteed misinformation, anxiety and needless, lasting guilt."

9

Government as Censor

The United States government does not censor; it puts no *imprimatur* (Latin for "let it be printed") on the written word or on any other form of expression, be it written, oral, visual, or any artistic shape or mode. Yet, as we shall see, the government *does* have the power to censor; it can pass judgment on certain forms of expression and it can, and on occasion has, indulged in censorship—meaning that *under some circumstances* the First Amendment has not always prevailed.

Take the case of the book, *The CIA and the Cult of Intelligence*, and try reading this:

DELETED

) *In actual practice, however, whatever damage was caused by the chemical was quickly repaired by the Vietcong and North Vietnamese.*

Now this:

At another meeting in 1970 the special discussion was on whether or not a very sophisticated satellite should be targeted against the (DELETED) part of the (DELETED) instead of (DELETED). The Air Force's request to (DELETED) its satellite came to the USIB under its responsibility for setting intelligence-collection priorities; citing the great cost of the satellite and the possibility that the (DELETED) might lead to a malfunction, the USIB said no to the (DELETED).

All of the "deleted" notations—there are 168 of them in the Victor Marchetti and John D. Marks book—were caused by the Central Intelligence Agency, which, upon

Manuscript pages of the CIA-censored book, *The CIA and the Cult of Intelligence. (Martha Kaplan)*

court order, reviewed the entire manuscript of the book prior to publication. Claiming the protection of national security, the CIA at first ordered the cutting of 339 passages of different lengths—15 to 20 percent of the manuscript—but then, upon demands of the authors' legal counsel, it agreed to reduce the number of deletions to 168.

In the meantime, the authors and the book's publisher, Alfred A. Knopf, sued the CIA in an effort to eventually get the entire book published.

Marchetti, who served for fourteen years with the CIA and said he wrote the book out of a desire to press for some reform of the United States intelligence system, accused the CIA and the government of trying to discourage him from writing the book in the first place and, subsequently, of trying to stop its publication. "They have managed," he says in the book's Preface, "through legal technicalities and by raising the specter of 'national security' violations, to achieve an unprecedented abridgment of my constitutional right to free speech. They have secured an unwarranted and outrageous *permanent* injunction against me, requiring that anything I write or say, '*factual, fictional or otherwise*,' on the subject of intelligence must first be censored by the CIA. Under risk of criminal contempt of court, I can speak only at my own peril and must allow the CIA thirty days to review, and excise, my writings—prior to submitting them to a publisher for consideration."

Marks, an analyst and staff assistant to the Intelligence Director of the State Department before joining Marchetti on the book in 1972, added that he entered the project "in the hope that what we have to say will have some effect in influencing the public and the Congress to institute meaningful control over American intelligence and to end the type of intervention abroad which, in addition to being counter-productive, is inconsistent with the ideals by which our country is supposed to govern itself."

In upholding the censorship of the book, lawyers for the government told U.S. District Court Judge Albert V. Bryan, Jr., in 1972 that while working at the CIA Marchetti had signed a number of "secrecy agreements," or contracts, binding him not to reveal anything of what he was exposed to while serving as an agent. Publication of his book, the lawyers argued, would result in "grave and irreparable injury to the interests of the United States."

Thus began an agonizing legal battle that stretched on for years, ending only toward the end of 1975 when the Supreme Court refused, for the second time, to review a United States Court of Appeals decision that forbade the authors from disclosing classified information about the CIA.

While the case was being fought in the courts, Marchetti had indicated he would risk imprisonment. "I might be willing, under certain circumstances, to stand up for the principles I believe in by going to jail," he stated. "If it would serve a useful purpose in breaking the government's censorship and get people to put pressure on Congress and so forth, it might be worth serving a nominal prison term."

The CIA's reaction to the book, added Marks, "shows what happens when you have government censorship. We won't be happy with any substantial cuts in the book."

After the first High Court rejection, Melvin L. Wulf, the legal director for the American Civil Liberties Union (ACLU), characterized the move as "a great defeat for Marchetti, for his lawyers—and for the First Amendment."

The Marchetti case—which has been called the "Pentagon Papers case of the publishing industry"—was unprecedented. Never before had the U.S. government exercised *prior restraint*—allowing censorship *previous* to publication. It also produced the first court test of CIA classification procedures, for along the way the authors did win a few victories of sorts. The CIA was ordered to prove that it had rightly classified its information as threatening national security, and to allow expert witnesses to examine the uncensored manuscript.

But overall it was a great defeat for civil libertarians and the publishing industry.

Wulf accused the CIA of using "the contract theory as a device for trying to suppress his book before it was put into print . . . it cheapens the First Amendment to say that an agreement by an employee of the United States not to reveal some government activity is the same as an agreement to deliver a hundred bales of cotton. It ignores the compelling democratic principle that the public has a right to be well informed about its government's actions."

Even though Marchetti was disclosing secrets, Wulf

said, he was not doing anything that many other high government officials have not done in their memoirs. The practice is harmless and, in fact, *valuable*, "because it provides the public with important information that it must have in order to pass judgment on its elected officials."

In its futile bid to have the High Court reconsider its decision not to review the case, the authors and the publisher said in a petition filed in 1975:

This case involves public issues which have been the subject of debate—often rancorous and divisive debate—over the past three years. Those issues include whether the state, in the name of national security, may engage secretly in activities through the electoral process: whether officials of the state, in the name of national security, may undertake virtually at whim to declare certain information to be "classified" and thus withhold it from the public; whether the same officials, in the name of national security, may trample upon First Amendment principles in order to suppress publication of information which they have unilaterally and arbitrarily declared to be secret; and whether these acts can be sustained against the weight of the First Amendment without, at the very least, the clearest and most explicit Congressional authorization.

Taking up the challenge, the Authors League of America cited the Marchetti case in urging Congress to con-

sider new legislation that would guarantee former
federal employees freedom of speech and press without
forcing them to press for these rights in costly court
cases. Writing to Rep. Robert W. Kastenmeier (D.,
Wis.) and Rep. William S. Moorhead (D., Pa.), Authors
League counsel Irwin Karp declared: "We believe that
a legislative examination now of the attempt to censor
the Marchetti book would be helpful in formulating
new legislation to protect valuable sources of information
for the public—books by former public employees—
against suppression and mutilation by the very agencies
and officials these publications seek to discuss and criticize."

During the unsuccessful battle for an uncensored
version of the Marchetti book, Knopf attorney Floyd
Abrams had likened the case to another example of
government censorship—the Pentagon Papers case. He
had asserted, as had been done for the *New York Times*
which published the Pentagon Papers without government approval, that censorship was justified only when
publication would "surely result in direct, immediate
and irreparable injury to the nation or its people."

The courts disagreed, holding that contracts involving
classified material are binding. While both cases do
represent examples of government censorship, there is
an important difference between the two. That is, both
the *Times* and the *Washington Post* published the controversial Pentagon Papers *before* any prior restraint
had been exercised. Why didn't Marchetti follow that
example and publish before going to court? Because,

) years later, he was elected mayor of West Berlin. Throughout this period, (

DELETED

) He was a hard-working politician in Allied-occupied Berlin, and his goal of making the Social Democratic party a viable alternative to communism (

DELETED

) And that evening after dinner, singer Pearl Bailey entertained the White House crowd in the East Room. The *Washington Post* reported the next day that she had "rocked" the White House. (

Page of the CIA-censored book, *The CIA and the Cult of Intelligence*. (Gerald S. Snyder, with permission from Alfred A. Knopf)

Marchetti has explained, in his case the prior restraint was aimed at him personally. He chose to see things out beforehand in the courts, for to do otherwise would make him liable for criminal charges resulting from violating the secrecy agreements he made with the CIA.

Because of its importance to the issue of censorship, the Pentagon Papers case bears looking at more closely. The case began on June 13, 1971, when a government employee named Daniel Ellsberg turned over to the *Times* papers containing a secret study the Pentagon was preparing about United States policy in Vietnam. These papers, Ellsberg contended, were needed by the nation to help the people evaluate the war, which he felt was immoral and unjust. But the government arrested Ellsberg and an accomplice, Anthony J. Russo, and charged them with espionage, theft, and conspiracy. During their trial in April 1973 it was revealed that Ellsberg's psychiatrist's office had been burglarized by the White House's so-called "Plumbers" unit in 1971, in order to secure evidence that could be used against Ellsberg in his trial. The judge accused the government of misconduct, stopped the trial, and dismissed all charges against Ellsberg and Russo.

In what sense had the government tried to "censor" the once-secret Pentagon Papers?

There can be no doubt that the Nixon administration tried to suppress the publication of the papers, and when the Supreme Court permitted their publication, it was saying, in effect, that the government had no right to keep from the public information which could do no "irreparable injury" to the people.

If, using the broadest interpretation of the meaning of censorship, it may be said that a secret, closed society is a censored society, and a censored society represents the total antithesis of the democratic concept, then governmental secrecy and governmental censorship come down to the same thing—the suppression of information. The government was trying to censor the Pentagon Papers.

But how, it can be argued, is the government to keep its secrets if it does not censor what it thinks the public should know?

The answer, the gut reaction of civil libertarians, is not that the government should not have secrets, but that the *burden of proof* should not be on those who wish to reveal some bit of delicate information; the burden, the libertarians contend, should be on those who wish to keep that information secret—on the government, in other words, and not on the people.

This generally was the argument put forth by the lawyers for Marchetti and Marks in the *CIA and the Cult of Intelligence* case. It is the argument of those who—in the light of the Pentagon Papers case, the aborted Ellsberg trial, the revelations of government abuse as brought out in the Watergate scandal, and the recent disclosures of secret spying by the CIA and the FBI—say that the government must turn its back on secrecy and move toward a more open society.

The Pentagon Papers and Marchetti disputes sharpened the debate over government censorship, and moved New York Congressman Jonathan B. Bingham to send to the House Judiciary Subcommittee on Civil and Constitutional Rights a "freedom of speech act of 1975" that would limit "prior restraint" on freedom of speech or press. In introducing the legislation, the New York Democratic-Liberal said he could see the need to suppress "certain military information," but that prior restraint should only take place in situations where "the government has both alleged and proved that communication of such matter will surely result in direct, immediate and irreparable damage to the security of the United States or its people."

In the past, prior censorship always had been a special vice in the minds of Supreme Court Justices. Former Chief Justice Earl Warren spoke for many when he said: "The censor performs free from all the procedural safeguards afforded litigants in a court of law." Committed to basic libertarian values, the Warren Court expressed its opposition to any system of prior restraint. The Warren Court more liberal than the present Burger Court, which has been more conservative than any of its predecessors—did not categorically reject the constitutionality of all censorship, but upheld censorship only where allegedly offensive material was given prompt and careful examination. It had great difficulty defining what the federal and state governments had the right to censor.

Yet for years, governments have had an "urge" to censor, born of a desire to protect "national security." In 1973 and 1974, the Nixon Administration drafted a secrecy-protecting bill (S. 1400) in response to the Pentagon Papers case. It was immediately attacked as an Official Secrets Act, such as exists in Great Britain.

Maine's Senator Edmund Muskie branded the proposed legislation a "peacetime . . . system of government censorship that a government could hardly tolerate in a time of war."

Hearings were held on the bill, and it was assumed it was dead, but then, in January 1975, in the Ford Administration, the same concept, slightly modified, reappeared when advocates of tighter government security moved to get through the Senate one of the most complicated pieces of legislation in American history: the controversial S. 1. This is a 750-page bill that would reform the nation's criminal laws. The need for criminal reform generally has been praised throughout the country, but proponents of freedom of speech and press have been quick to point out and criticize several provisions that would make it a crime to publish "national defense information."

Under the provisions of such a bill, the government, in effect, would have the right of censorship over certain information. This, in the view of the critics, would bring the United States close to establishing an Official Secrets Act, and would raise serious threats to First Amendment protections.

If such a bill had been in effect in 1971, when *The New York Times* and *Washington Post* published the Pentagon Papers, the government would have had a case for prosecuting those newspapers.

"On a dangerously broad and ill-defined scale," noted the *Washington Star*, in criticizing S. 1,. "reporters receiving 'unauthorized' information on national defense and other matters could face criminal prosecution. It could hush up the discussion, on any informed basis, of some of the largest and gravest public matters. It is alien to our constitutional guarantee of free press and free speech, and even to consider such a repressive move on the 200th anniversary of the Republic is highly odious."

Shouldn't there be some sort of gag on the inner doings of government? The government security advocates say yes, but those opposed assert that once any form of government censorship takes hold, all kinds of coverups may take place under the label of "national security." Observed the *Star* in protest of S. 1: "Some of the worst boondoggles and misdeeds might never have been known had not some public-spirited employes or former employes of government made available the facts that higher-ups wanted to keep hidden."

In the words of Arthur J. Moore, writing in the August 18, 1975, *Christianity and Crisis:* "Our pressing need at the moment is to demythologize government operations, and this can best be done by openness. . . . Such generalized rationales for secrecy as 'national security' need to be abandoned in favor of concrete spelling out of consequences. Coupled with this must be constant reminders that we all tend to magnify both the importance and the delicacy of our work. Secrecy won't do and must continuously be opposed as the conditions which bring it into being continuously reappear. For some of us will care, and somehow most of us will get things into some kind of context, and, most important of all, someone will appear from time to time to tell the rest of us that we aren't wearing any clothes."

Throughout this book we have seen scattered examples of alleged government censorship attempts. But nothing was more disturbing than the story that made news toward the end of 1975. At that time, it was disclosed that for years the CIA illegally opened the mail of "selected American politicians," including Edward Kennedy, Hubert Humphrey, Frank Church, Martin Luther King, Richard Nixon, and hundreds of other persons.

Hundreds of thousands of pieces of mail were examined and opened in a blatant example of invasion of privacy. It is a violation of the law to open mail. The intercepted letters were not actually "censored," in the strict sense of the word. That is, the information in the letters was not actually suppressed. But part of the censorship process—the *examination* of possible objec-

20   I SAW THE FALL OF THE PHILIPPINES

ica, all the nations in the Far East are here to exploit us. That exploitation will not end until one of our own colored peoples assumes leadership. It is suicide for us to oppose the leadership of Japan."

Everywhere I went I heard talk in favor of Japan—among the natives. The fifth-column work of the Japanese had been

American military censors in World War II blacked out parts of Carlos P. Romulo's book, *I Saw the Fall of the Philippines*. (Gerald S. Snyder, with permission from Harold Matson Company)

tionable material—was carried out, and the CIA agents assumed the pose of censors.

Not only letters but international cables were intercepted and read and sometimes photographed by government monitors. A House subcommittee headed by New York Congresswoman Bella Abzug said a staff investigation revealed that for thirty years cable traffic in the Washington offices of RCA Global Communication and ITT World Communications was examined by the FBI.

Senator Frank Church, the Idaho Democrat who is chairman of the Senate Intelligence Committee, said that even a letter he wrote to his mother-in-law was found by investors in the CIA's files. For 26 years— from 1940 to 1966—it was revealed that the CIA had a mail intercept program that involved a "Watch List" containing some 1,300 names. In addition, the mail of many prominent American citizens not on the list was opened, photographed, and put back into the mail, with copies going to CIA headquarters in Washington, D.C.

The CIA did not deny the opening of certain Americans' mail, nor did it deny that this was illegal. But it did defend its actions as vital to national security. "From a counterintelligence point of view," said former CIA counterintelligence chief James Angleton, who directed the mail opening program from 1955 to 1973, "it was vitally important to know everything possible about contacts between U.S. citizens and Communist countries."

But little evidence was produced to show that the

mail intercept program had been successful. When Fritz Schwarz, the Intelligence Committee counsel, asked William Branigan, the chief of the FBI section which received information from the CIA, if a single foreign agent had been arrested as a result of the program, Branigan responded, "To my knowledge, no."

The opening of Church's letter to his mother-in-law, sent while the senator was on a trip to the Soviet Union in 1974, inspired the humorist Art Buchwald to take up the theme in a column that, in part, went like this:

> *I came home the other night from work, and I saw a man sitting on my stoop steaming open my mail.*
>
> *"Hey, what the heck are you doing?" I demanded.*
>
> *He took out his wallet and flashed a card. "I'm from the CIA. I'm just checking to see if you're getting many letters from the Iron Curtain countries."*
>
> *"You're not supposed to open people's mail," I said. "That's illegal . . . And why are you steaming open a letter from my mother-in-law?"*
>
> *". . . Aha, you say it's from your mother-in-law, but we know the other side always corresponds with its agents through a mother-in-law."*

Yet despite any fun we might poke at the CIA, or any other government agency, the government, remember, is not a censor. Thanks to the First Amendment, the courts have moved continuously to protect all forms of expression and are—despite the examples of censorship in this chapter—extremely sensitive to the dangers inherent in any form of government censorship. The Supreme Court voiced it well, for instance, when in mid-1975, in striking down an ordinance prohibiting drive-in theaters from showing films containing nudity on screens visible from public places, the Court said ". . . . when the government, acting as censor, undertakes selectively to shield the public from some kinds of speech on the ground that they are more offensive than others, the First Amendment strictly limits its power. Such selective restrictions have been upheld only when the speaker intrudes on the privacy of the home, or the degree of captivity makes it impractical for the unwilling viewer or auditor to avoid exposure."

Justice Lewis F. Powell, Jr., who wrote this majority opinion (in *Erznoznik v. City of Jacksonville*), observed that a great deal of what is found today offends "our esthetic, if not our political and moral, sensibilities." Nevertheless, he asserted, "The Constitution does not permit the government to decide which types of otherwise protected speech are sufficiently offensive to require protection for the unwilling listener or viewer."

The government is by and large our protector against infringement of First Amendment freedoms. Censorious restraints upon freedom of speech and expression, while not unheard of, are bound at one time or another to come up against the famous words adopted some 185 years ago: "Congress shall make no laws . . ."

10

What's Ahead?
The Future of Censorship

Imagine, if you can, the ultimate horror of censorship, where in some future society books put to the torch become flesh and blood and cry out! In the Ray Bradbury novella *Fahrenheit 451,* a character discusses the notion of the death of knowledge:

We are all bits and pieces of history and literature and international law, Byron, Tom Paine, Machiavelli or Christ, it's here. And the hour's late. And the war's begun . . . All we want to do is keep the knowledge we think we will need, intact and safe. We're not out to incite or anger anyone yet. For if we are destroyed the knowledge is dead, perhaps for good. We are model citizens, in our own special way; we walk the old tracks, we lie in the hills at night, and the city people let us be. We're stopped and searched occasionally, but there's nothing on our persons to incriminate us. The organization is flexible, very loose, and fragmentary. Some of us have had plastic surgery on our faces and fingerprints. Right now we have a horrible job; we're waiting for the war to begin and, as quickly, end. It's not pleasant, but then we're not in control, we're the odd minority crying in the wilderness. When the war's over, perhaps we can be of some use in the world.

Frightening, yes; unbelievable, perhaps; but the ultimate horror of censorship would be the death of knowledge—a situation in which, as a book-burning fireman named Montag says in the book, there is "one generation printing, another generation burning, yet another remembering what is good to remember so as to print again."

As extreme as this example is, it does serve to point up the fright felt by some civil libertarians over the threat posed by any form of censorship. Books can never become flesh and blood, they say, but knowledge can be destroyed.

On the other hand, declare those who argue for tougher censorship laws for America, it is not the threat to future knowledge but the threat to future morality that is at stake. Writing in the magazine *The Progressive*, public opinion specialist Reo M. Christenson asserted that the American people are:

> . . . affronted by books, magazines, movies, plays, erotic displays, pictures, and records which vulgarize, desecrate, and cheapen sex, or which encourage or glamorize deviant sexual behavior. The

Middle American—and many others— have a deep-rooted suspicion that all of this will undermine certain moral restraints believed to be essential to the public weal. There is no way of proving whether this suspicion is or is not well-founded. But the public's fears about excessive sexual permissiveness are supported more than they are challenged by such inadequate empirical evidence that we have . . . A society can tolerate only so much emotional turmoil, so much disruption, so many assaults upon its sensibilities and its mores. At some point, the public's patience becomes exhausted; it cries, "Enough." This denouement may not be far off in America. For the record, I find much to applaud in our revolutionary age: the refusal to support a senseless war; the challenge to the military budget and to certain military assumptions; the so-called "equality revolution;" the demand for justice to the blacks and the poor; the call for sweeping educational reforms; the insistence on higher standards of public morality. But the stresses and strains involved in these movements are hard enough for the body politic to bear. Add to these a dubious sexual revolution powerfully stimulated by the entertainment industry, and society may be bearing an overload of tension.

Whether current tensions are the reason or not, the signs are everywhere that far more, not less, censorship is in the immediate future. As the trend continues toward increased freedom of views in all forms of communication—newspapers, movies, books, magazines, television—expressions of artistic and social values can be expected to become more open. And this, in turn, is apt to continue to provoke those who cling to the old values, who still want a return to "the good old days, where right was right and wrong was wrong," where the notions of mother and church were inviolate, and whoever spoke out against them was held to be speaking out against God and against everything that was good.

As more and more innovative programs are introduced into the school systems, these are bound to provoke the ire of those parents who continue to rebel against the desire to do things differently from when they were students. What has happened to the "traditional values," what's wrong with the "good old-fashioned American goals" of yesteryear, they are apt to ask in the future. For many, the switch to new ways, the acceptance of entirely different sets of values, may be enough to set into the open a deep-rooted dread of intellectualism and fear of education and teachers. It is easy to see how the search for truth, the continuing inquiring by inquiring minds will likely upset traditional values and anger those who hold these values dear.

As for the students themselves, it seems only realistic to expect that in the future they will want more, not fewer, of the books that reveal the very real world around them. Their enthusiasm for reading about and seeing the truth of things is much more likely to increase than diminish. How else, except through books, the critics of censorship maintain, can students best learn to see and understand themselves and their problems, and view the lives and problems of other people in other places? If the arguments for literature need to be explained to a future generation, it could probably not be put more eloquently than by Dr. Ken Donelson of the Department of English at Arizona State University, who has said: "Literature allows young people to see themselves and their problems perhaps a little more objectively; literature provides vicarious experiences beyond the possibilities of any one person's life; literature frees students to meet other people in other places and other times, to see similarities and differences between people, and to meet a multitude of human, moral, and physical dilemmas; literature exposes young people to value systems and ideas and practices different from their own, which can lead to an assessment of both the students' values and those of other people; literature allows students to discover the world as it was and as it is, a world neither all good nor all evil, but a world all human; and above all, that literature provides deep enjoyment and satisfaction."

The censors of the future might readily say they agree to this, but they might still argue that much of what future librarians and teachers of English see as literature is not really "literature" at all, but "filth," or "anti-Christian" material, or "un-American" matter, or "pornography," or "right-wing trash."

No matter what happens, controversy seems certain; and the frequency of this controversy is apt to increase in intensity for other reasons. For one thing, sexual attitudes seem to be heading for even more dramatic change, for less and less constriction, more and more humanism.

There is no telling how far things will go, but those who see the trend are already prone to call any move toward more sexual freedom a very healthy sign, arguing that in the past people have been too guilt-laden and frightened about sex. In the words of one psychiatrist: "The advantages far outweigh the disadvantages because we are beginning to see that sex is a normal human function which should be enjoyed; it is being removed from the historic burden of guilt, shame, and fear. This will lessen the enormous number of sexual problems we see."

The psychiatrist continued: "I think if the new humanism in sex continues, in a generation or two there will be far less sexual problems. The news media and communications are spreading the new humanism about sexuality which will make it easier for people to enjoy sex without guilt or fear. I ought to be out of business in two generations."

In two generations, however, who is to say that sexual liberation will not be overdone? If it is overdone, might this be to such an extent that people will be pushed by sexual pressures? If this happens, the protest of those who simply have had enough can be expected to be heard; rightly or wrongly, they may be labeled as "censors," but they will condemn the new sexual liberation, calling it a trend toward complete promiscuity, a move toward compulsive sexuality.

All of this, of course, deals with what *might* happen; there is no real way to predict the future. But looking closer at what may happen, or at what the signs seem to indicate will happen, let's consider the various possible outlooks: the short-term, mid-term, and long-term.

Short-term: Nineteen seventy-six is an election year, and in election years, maintain the censorship watchers, there is much more local and state censorship "rabble-rousing" among office holders or seekers.

As evidence of this, one observer pointed to the reams of obscenity legislation now pending all over the United States, and termed this an "overwhelming" problem for the publishing industry, which is continuously being challenged for publishing "dirty books."

For another view on the short-term outlook, consider this: "The anti-obscenity, anti-pornography emotions appear to have abated at least temporarily, partly as a result of Watergate and subsequent scandals and partly, in my opinion, as a result of the economic decline. These problems just seem more important to people than hard or soft core pornography."

Generally speaking, it is the view of the anticensorship forces that the censorship movement and the feelings of state and local authorities have been set back by the revelations and consequences of Watergate in 1974, and by the revelations in 1975 of CIA corporate political pay-offs and payments. Thus, the issue of secrecy and/or censorship is now out in the open again for a full discussion, and that is seen as a healthy sign.

Mid-term: "That's the problem in my opinion," says Robert Gutwillig of the Playboy Press. "Because of the conservatively-oriented Supreme Court, the likelihood of more conservative appointments, the reality of other conservative appointees filling other federal judicial vacancies, the courts could well prove difficult for the next 10-15 years. Frankly, I am not altogether enthusiastic about sending up more important censorship issues to the Supreme Court. In the event of a Democratic Presidential victory next fall, we may want to review the situation. But it doesn't look good now."

There is no reason to believe that, ten years from now, fundamentalist Christians will revise their cultural outlook. They are apt to continue to fear that their moralistic views are being undermined by secular public education. They are just as apt to believe then that their own pietistic way of life is adequate, and that attempts to show "life as it is" are slights, or condescending attempts, against their faith, initiated by schools, bureaucrats, and the upper classes in general.

Might it be that, ten years from now, the urgings of fundamentalist Christians will be "fashionable," just as the issues advanced today by the feminists are so deemed?

It is impossible to answer this question today. Yet in the future, as at least one observer sees it, "the working class is not going to put up indefinitely with sophisticated scorn of its values. It might help defuse similar situations if the educated elite were to recognize that, in spite of the inarticulate and excessive nature of the protest, the Kanawha County parents had a point."

As for the offending books, there is little reason to believe that they will be much different ten years from now. For one thing, books don't change overnight. School books remain in use for three to five years before they are replaced, and it takes a great deal of time for books to be written, edited, and marketed.

"Despite all the current hopes, slogans and trends," noted one observer of the education scene, "schools won't be too much different in ten years from what they are now. The books and materials currently in production will predominate in the schools. And ten years from now, about 75 percent of the teachers around today will still be around."

Don't look for a radical change in the way things are. Do look for positive changes which may come from the growing experience of peoples of different social and cultural backgrounds learning to live together; they should be expected to better tolerate and respect one another. But the basic problems, of which the question of censorship is just one, will very likely remain.

Long-Term: The concensus among the anticensorship forces is that time and changing mores are on their side. Looking to the long view—and by "long" they generally mean about twenty-five years—they view the immediate signs as gradually shifting to embrace the liberal, controversial attitudes of today.

The Supreme Court made its *Miller* ruling on the basis of tastes and standards as it saw them in 1973. As tastes and standards change, the opinions of the Court also can be expected to shift. At the same time, as the makeup of the Court changes, from the present middle-aged or elderly Justices of the upper middle-class, to younger and more liberal Justices, it can be expected to find the so-called obscene material not to be in such "bad taste" as their predecessors found it. The actions of the present Court reflect traditional middle-class distaste for vulgarity and bad taste. The more liberal members would agree with Justice Douglas, who said: "The Court is at large because we deal with tastes and standards of literature. What shocks me may be sustenance for my neighbors. What causes this person to boil up in rage over one pamphlet or movie may reflect only his neurosis, not shared by others. We deal here with problems of censorship which, if adopted, should be done by constitutional amendment after full debate."

Speaking on liberty and obscenity at a lecture sponsored by the National Endowment for the Humanities, Paul A. Freund, an eminent constitutional scholar, predicted that in the future obscenity laws will not create the stir they do now. Noting that "no area of law is less satisfactory than this one," the Harvard law professor said that in the future a great deal of what is now viewed as obscene "may be adjudged a sin against language or an offense against art," but it will not be the crime it now is.

Gradually, he said, the law will change: "My judgment is that the law will come to confine itself to public displays, on the analogy of public nuisances; to distribution to juveniles, as an adjunct to parental control, and to zoning restrictions for theaters and bookstores specializing in this form of popular culture."

The signs are already here, he says, since judgments on obscene material are more and more coming to be based on the work as a whole and not on isolated passages, and people—and courts—are coming to frown on claims that a work of art is obscene just because someone sees it as "immoral."

Freund's views are seen as being in line with Supreme Court views today, but *minority* views. And minority views are not about to become majority views overnight, as Freund notes. It will take time for the Supreme Court to change, and if change does come about, with the Court moving toward the position of the minority, it may be because it sees that its latest decisions affecting obscenity have created more problems than they have solved. As some observers have pointed out, the Supreme Court majority does not necessarily reflect the views of the majority of people in the country, as evidenced by the fact that juries across the nation have shown a reluctance to convict in obscenity cases.

Freund ended his lecture on a note of optimism: "Generation by generation, struggle by struggle, we in America—writers and speakers, politicians and artists— have achieved at least for a historical moment a degree of freedom from official control that would, I dare say, amply gratify Milton, Locke, Mill and Thomas Jefferson."

Others also see the future as bright. How nice it would be, said one anticensorship advocate, "if we were able to celebrate our 200th birthday as a nation in 1976 with the same obscenity laws we had when this nation was founded: namely, no obscenity laws directed against sex at all—with freedom, in other words, from the fear of sex which is really what underlies the obscenity laws and which subverts our First Freedom." This is not apt to happen, of course, not in 1976, or 1986, or beyond. The struggle of people to live free of the peril of censorship will continue. But the safeguard provided by the First Amendment will never be lost. It will always remain the right of all Americans, the first right, the right upon which all other rights exist: the right to be informed.

BIBLIOGRAPHY

Carlsen, G. Robert. *Books and the Teen-age Reader.* New York: Harper & Row, 1971.

Commission on Obscenity and Pornography. *The Report of the Commission on Obscenity and Pornography.* Washington, D.C.: U.S. Government Printing Office, 1970.

Corwin, Edward S. *The Constitution and What It Means Today.* Princeton: Princeton University Press, 1974.

Friedman, Leon, ed. *Obscenity: The Complete Oral Arguments Before the Supreme Court in the Major Obscenity Cases.* New York: Chelsea House, 1970.

Haight, Anne Lyon. *Banned Books.* New York: Bowker, 1970.

Hoyt, Olga, and Hoyt, Edwin. *Censorship in America.* New York: Seabury, 1970.

Kaye, Evelyn. *The Family Guide to Children's Television.* New York: Pantheon, 1974.

Kraenkel, Osmond K. *The Supreme Court and Civil Liberties.* New York: Oceana, 1960.

Kristol, Irving. *Where Do You Draw the Line?* Provo, Utah: Brigham Young University Press, 1971.

Levine, Alan, with Cary, Eve, and Divoky, Diane. *The Rights of Students.* New York: Avon, 1973.

Liston, Robert. *The Right To Know.* New York: Watts, 1973.

Mott, Frank Luther. *American Journalism.* New York: Macmillan, 1950.

Norwick, Kenneth P. *Lobbying for Freedom.* New York: St. Martin's Press, 1975.

Rubin, David. *The Rights of Teachers.* New York: Avon, 1972.

Schumach, Murray. *The Face on the Cutting Room Floor.* New York: Da Capo Press, 1964.

Sex Information and Education Council of the U.S. (SIECUS). *Sexuality and Man.* New York: Scribner's, 1970.

Snyder, Gerald S. *The Right To Be Let Alone: Privacy in the United States.* New York: Julian Messner, 1975.

ABOUT THE AUTHOR

Gerald S. Snyder was born and grew up in New York City, and holds a Bachelor of Journalism degree from the University of Missouri. He has freelanced from Europe and North Africa, and for more than four years was a member of the news staff of United Press International in New York. In 1971, after almost five years as a staff writer for the National Geographic Society in Washington, D.C., he turned to full-time freelancing.

The Right To Be Informed is Mr. Snyder's eighth book and follows *The Right To Be Let Alone: Privacy in the United States.* His other books have covered a wide range of subjects, including computers, religion, the study of the future, and American history. He resides in Silver Spring, Maryland, with his wife, Arlette, and two children, a daughter, Michele, and a son, Daniel.

+098.120973   Pi 77 15040
Sn92r   729
Snyder
The right to be informed

JUN 9 1984
JUL 1 6 1985

OCC8111HC80 / SHC77-79   c 76